Canoeing and Kayaking

Canoeing and Kayaking

Wolf Ruck

McGraw-Hill Ryerson Limited

Toronto   Montreal   New York   London   Sydney
Johannesburg   Mexico   Panama   Düsseldorf
Singapore   São Paulo   Kuala Lumpur   New Delhi

Canoeing and Kayaking
Copyright© McGraw-Hill Ryerson Limited, 1974.

Illustrations and Photography by W.E. Ruck.
Photographs by Barbara Shaw
on pages 46, 47, 48, 90 and 92.

ISBN 0-07-077761-6

Library of Congress Catalog Card Number 73-21369

2 3 4 5 6 7 8 9 0 BP 1 0 9 8 7 6

ACKNOWLEDGEMENTS

For their encouragement and wealth of expert knowledge, I
would like to express my sincere appreciation to: Professor Kirk
Wipper and the staff of Camp Kandalore, whose enthusiastic
expertise has for many years advanced the idea of paddling
excellence in Canada; members past and present of the Missis-
sauga Canoe Club of Port Credit, whose renown in competitive
circles is paddling history; and the many paddling friends and
acquaintances whose interest and readiness to impart their skill
and share their experience will continue to open new vistas to
the interested paddler and win new friends for this enjoyable
sport.
For their skill and patience in demonstrating technique, I am
especially indebted to Gabor Joo, Les Reithauser, John Wood,
Scott Lee, Joanna Wipper and Barbara Shaw.
A word of thanks also to the editorial staff and art department
of McGraw-Hill Ryerson, Toronto, whose technical and artistic
advice proved an immeasurable aid to the diagrammatic and
photographic renditions.

W. E. R.

Printed and bound in Canada

CONTENTS

FOREWORD BY KIRK A. W. WIPPER

Co-founder of the National Canoe Schools
Director of Camp Kandalore
Director of the Heritage Trail including the
    Museum of Canoes and Kayaks of North America
Professor, School of Physical and Health Education,
    University of Toronto

North Americans have recently become more aware of their heritage in which the indigenous canoe and kayak played a most important role. Without those frail craft which carried explorer, fur trader, missionary, surveyor, engineer, prospector, ranger and trapper, the development of this continent could have taken a very different course. No wonder that modern wilderness travellers can identify with a glorious past when their paddles are dipped along the same waterways plied by our rugged forefathers.

Today, more and more people are discovering the pleasures to be found in the sports of canoeing and kayaking. A paddler may choose to travel a peaceful, serene route, or he may relish the adventure and excitement of challenging turbulent waters or competing in races. Above all, paddling is a superb way of enjoying the outdoors without disrupting its natural beauty and harmony.

In a time when physical fitness is regarded as a serious national problem, the value of canoeing and kayaking becomes especially significant. There is no doubt that recreational touring and competitive paddling contribute measurably to the fitness of the participants.

This timely manual presents the essential information needed by the rapidly growing numbers of people who are taking up the art and science of paddling. May they use it well and pursue their paddling interests with confidence and joy.

Kirk A. W. Wipper

Chapter 1   Canoes and Kayaks

CHOOSING A CRAFT

The paddler should choose a craft whose design elements and handling characteristics best suit his needs. If his interest lies mainly in recreational paddling, an all-purpose craft which handles reasonably well in a variety of water conditions is most appropriate. The touring enthusiast will consider the number of paddlers and the amount of equipment to be carried as well as the type of water anticipated en route — the open waters of coastal regions or large inland lakes, lakes and rivers with occasional rapids, or mainly white water. If frequent or extended portages form part of the route, he would do well to examine the craft's portability in terms of weight and comfort on the shoulders of the carrier.

For the white water (WW) and flat water (FW) racing competitor, only the most highly evolved and specialized racing shell will be suitable.

Another basic choice remains — canoe or kayak? While there are definite similarities between canoe and kayak in paddling principles and techniques, one craft may have a decided advantage over the other under certain conditions. Also, some paddlers simply prefer either canoe *or* kayak, while others find equal enjoyment in *both*.

For the beginner, it is perhaps best to keep an open mind and learn to enjoy the attributes of both. For the seasoned paddler, it is always an enlightening experience to paddle a less familiar craft.

Canoes

The canoe was invented by the North American Indian and for many centuries served as the most versatile method of transportation in this land of countless interconnecting waterways. The typical canoe is characterized by an *open deck* and a "mirror-image" profile. It is normally propelled by means of a *single-blade* paddle. Large load capacity for paddlers and equipment, relative ease and comfort of portaging, good overview in rapids and adaptability for a variety of uses are some of its advantages.

On the other hand, an open canoe can swamp in high waves and the open *gunwales* (hull edges) are easily caught by crosscurrents which can capsize the craft in fast-flowing waters. The relatively high profile is susceptible to side-winds which can cause difficulties in holding course or making headway. Also, single-blade paddling is essentially *asymmetric* and requires a spe-

cialized technique to balance the one-sided application of forces. This often reduces speed and limits quick manoeuvring.

Kayaks

The kayak originated among the Eskimo peoples of the Arctic, who needed a speedy scouting and hunting craft suitable for use on large, open bodies of water. The *closed deck* and sealable *cockpit* make the kayak virtually unsinkable in the highest waves, and perfection of the Eskimo roll obviates the necessity of ejecting from a capsized boat — the prospect of having to swim for a distant shore offering slim chances for survival in Arctic waters. Its low profile makes it less susceptible than a canoe to side-winds, and the seated paddling position allows the use of a steering mechanism for added control. The *double-blade* kayak paddle results in a *symmetrical* paddling style which lends itself to quick and efficient application of forces on both sides. Swiftness and seaworthiness under extreme water conditions are special attributes of the kayak.

Kayaks have some disadvantages. They are essentially for singles paddling and have no room for extra passengers in an emergency. On a group tour, a weak or inexperienced paddler may be unable to maintain the pace or handle his boat in difficult water. On tours requiring frequent portaging, loading and unloading bulky equipment through small cockpits can prove frustrating. In addition, the low-slung kayak invariably gives a wet ride which calls for suitable clothing and special precautions in cold weather.

MATERIALS OF CONSTRUCTION

Today, the earliest canoes and kayaks made of bark and skin are found only in museums or occasionally in remote regions where the ready availability of these materials makes them practical for the inhabitants.

The modern-day equivalent of the Indian bark canoe is the *wood-canvas* (cedar-strip) canoe. The improvements made over its predecessor in durability and structural strength have been attained at the expense of increased weight — a disadvantage on portages and when the canoe must be handled by one person on land. The canvas skin is susceptible to tearing on sharp rocks and snags. The interior wood surfaces must be kept varnished and in good repair to prevent absorption of water, which would increase weight and eventually lead to dry-rot, weakening the structure. Nevertheless, the wood-canvas canoe probably offers the most aesthetically pleasing paddling experience to the recreational canoeist and the paddling connoisseur.

A resemblance to the Eskimo kayak is most obvious in the "foldboat" (folding kayak) which, for decades, has enjoyed widespread popularity, especially in Europe. The foldboat consists of a wood frame structure supporting a rubberized waterproof "skin." It is ingeniously designed to be disassembled, forming neat suitcase-size packages which may be stored and transported more easily than rigid hulls. Its overall weight, sensitive skin and limited design possibilities are, however, disadvantages in the light of more recent developments. Today, *aluminum* and *polyester-fibreglass* (P-F) have found increased use as canoe-building materials, and modern kayak hulls are almost all made of P-F. These materials offer resistance to abrasion, minimal maintenance requirements, ease of repair and considerable strength without excessive weight. Under impact, P-F has the unique property of resiliency to the breaking point — it springs back to its original shape — whereas aluminum may be dented and wood cracked under the same stress. Good P-F hulls are "laid up" by hand with different weight fibreglass cloth and matting combined and placed strategically for maximum strength with minimum thickness and weight. On the hull surface, a tough, resilient and extremely smooth gel coat increases durability and reduces drag due to friction.

The most significant advantage of P-F construction, however, lies in the relatively simple use of *moulds* which make feasible the duplication of very complex hull designs. In the sport of WW paddling, this had led to the extreme specialization of hull design which makes possible the spectacularly dynamic and effective WW techniques. Since the specific gravities of aluminum and P-F exceed that of water, a swamped hull will sink unless fitted with special *flotation* aids. Inflatable flotation bags or buoyant materials (such as styrofoam) sufficient to keep a swamped hull afloat are therefore standard equipment. These should be evenly apportioned between bow and stern so that the swamped hull floats level, facilitating control and rescue. Permanently sealed air compartments forming an integral part of the hull are less suitable, as the smallest leak will quickly nullify their effectiveness, add weight and upset the hull's balance.

The lightest and swiftest boats — the FW racing shells — are constructed of multi-ply mahogany / spruce veneer less than ⅛ inch thick. The smoothly varnished and extremely fragile shell requires utmost care in handling and maintenance. Scrapes, gouges and stove-ins occur readily on impact and raw, exposed surfaces absorb moisture which quickly leads to dry-rot. Some paddlers apply a hard floor wax to the hull surface to add protection and minimize drag due to friction. After each use, the exterior surface should be washed with a mild soap solution and rinsed with clean water, and the hull should be wiped dry, inside and out, with a clean cloth.

The shells are best stored in a moderately dry and warm location indoors. They should be stored right-side-up — especially the closed kayak hulls — to facilitate drying of the interior.

HULL DESIGN

Canoe and kayak hulls are designed with specific properties and handling qualities in mind. Touring craft must have sufficient volume to give the *buoyancy* required to carry heavy loads.

Stability — the resistance to capsizing — is desirable to some degree in all boats. Boats used mainly on fast-flowing water where tight, fast turns must be executed should turn easily — they require a high degree of *manoeuvrability*. When the aim is to cover a distance in the shortest time, *swiftness* is of primary importance. On flat, open waters where straight-line travel is most efficient, *directional stability* is a definite asset, and, when high waves are encountered, a measure of *rough water stability* is also helpful.

These characteristics are not always compatible: a hull designed for speed has little inherent stability or manoeuvrability, while a highly stable and manoeuvrable craft is not as fast as a racing shell. In general, the more specialized the purpose, the greater the emphasis on one specific handling quality, with a corresponding sacrifice of the others. Multi-purpose designs, on the other hand, should offer a reasonable compromise which allows the paddler to enjoy a wide range of paddling experiences.

The elements of hull design which determine the fundamental properties and handling characteristics of the craft are: hull dimensions; the shape of hull cross-sections, longitudinal formlines and keel-line; and, in closed hulls, the deck form.

Hull Dimensions

The longer, wider and deeper the hull, the greater its volume. Voluminous hulls have greater buoyancy and can carry heavier loads than smaller hulls. Long, narrow hulls are characteristically fast, hold a straight-line course well and, by spanning troughs and burrowing through the sides of high waves, maintain a stable, even-keeled ride. Short, wide hulls are very stable in the upright position and can be turned easily.

Hull Cross Sections

Most hulls are a combination of three basic cross-sectional forms, each of which contributes a share to the handling characteristics. In specialized hulls (e.g., racing shells) one form may predominate along most of the length. In all-purpose models, the bow portion may be formed for speed and directional stability, the mid-section for stability and the stern end for manoeuvrability.

Rectangular. Wide, flat-bottomed hulls with high sides are voluminous and buoyant. Stability is greatest when the hull is upright, but tends to *decrease* rapidly with lean and the capsizing point is reached abruptly. These hulls ride high in the water, minimizing resistance to turning and increasing manoeuvrability by sliding readily over the water surface.

V-shaped. V-hulls are very unstable in the upright position, but stability *increases* with lean onto the flat hull surface and the capsizing point is reached gradually.

They sit deep in the water, maximizing the resistance to turning and increasing directional stability.

Long, narrow V-hulls are very fast, but their inherent tippiness calls for good balance and paddling control.

Semicircular. The minimal inherent stability of semicircular hulls in the upright position does not change appreciably with lean.

They sit deep in the water but tend to rise slightly out of the water at high speed. This planing effect makes them somewhat faster than V-hulls in the hands of an expert.

Longitudinal Formlines

Fusiform. Fusiform hulls are typified by a *beam* (the widest part of the hull) located amidships and sides tapering symmetrically to a point at bow and stern. This is the basic design of most canoes and all-purpose kayaks.

The load can be evenly distributed towards bow and stern so that the *centre of gravity* (the point where the weight may be considered to be concentrated) is located amidships for good *trim* (balance) and control.

The streamlined shape gives a reasonably fast boat and the symmetrical distribution of volume in bow and stern portions gives a smooth, stable ride in all kinds of water.

Delta-form. Sometimes called the Swedish-form, the beam of the delta-hull is well behind amidships. Flat water racing and, more recently, white water racing canoes and kayaks are characteristically delta-forms.

The narrow hull adjacent to the paddler's position allows placement of propulsive strokes close to the *centre-line* (straight line from bow to stern), minimizing the turning effect for maximum forward speed.

The greater hull volume behind amidships is more sensitive to the effects

Fusiform

Delta-form

Fish-form

of side-winds and waves. Delta-hulls therefore tend to veer (yaw) easily off course.

Fish-form. The fish-form, in which the beam is located *ahead* of amidships, is sometimes seen in WW and all-purpose kayak hulls. The greater volume in the bow gives more stowage room and reduces the tendency of the bow to burrow into waves. This gives a drier ride as the hull follows the undulations of the water surface more closely.

In contrast to the delta-hull, the bow portion is more affected by side-winds

and waves, and the strokes must be placed further out from the centre-line, reducing the efficiency of forward propulsion.

The Keel-line

The keel-line is an imaginary line running along the middle of the hull bottom from bow to stern. It may be prominent, as in V-hulls, or largely imaginary, as in semicircular hulls.

Most canoes have either an attached or a built-in keel running along part of

the keel-line, the deeper *fin-keel* being more suited to deep waters and the flatter, wider *shoe-keel* offering better protection in shallow streams. So-called *bilge-keels* running along the rounded edge of a flat-bottomed hull serve no useful purpose when paddling. Their main function is to protect the hull on land, but their added weight and the diminished manoeuvrability they create make them undesirable for normal use. Whether resulting from hull shape or a built-in or attached keel, a deep, prominent keel-line always improves directional stability, especially in side-winds, and correspondingly reduces manoeuvrability.

Rocker

Viewed from the side, the keel-line may be straight or it may sweep up gradually towards bow and stern forming the *rocker.* The rocker allows the bow and stern to ride higher in the water, reducing resistance to turning.

The resulting manoeuvrability is most advantageous in WW boats where quick turning is required.

Excessive rocker is undesirable for flat water travel. The bow tends to rise on the *bow wave* and the resulting ''uphill'' ride is both strenuous and inefficient over long distances.

Low deck—rounded gunwales

Flat deck—edged gunwales

High deck—rounded gunwales

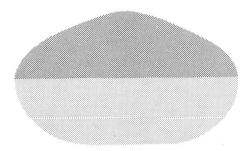

Ridged deck—edged gunwales

Deck Forms

All kayaks and WW canoes have closed hulls. The paddler assumes position in the *cockpit* — an opening in the deck. By means of a waterproof *spray-skirt,* the space between the paddler's body and the *coaming* (cockpit rim) can be sealed to water while not hampering freedom of movement. The hull can now be ploughed through high waves, leaned sharply on its side, submerged and even rolled over completely — all

without shipping a single drop of water. Decks may be high or low, and flat, ridged, or oval. The *gunwales* (where hull and deck meet) are correspondingly edged or rounded.

Bow and stern decks of one hull may differ, as in the delta-form where a high, oval deck maximizes volume for added buoyancy in the narrow bow portion and a low, flat deck minimizes undesirable volume in the wider stern. High decks have better water run-off

and the hull rides drier through waves. The increased volume adds buoyancy and stowage capacity for touring.

Low decks are less sensitive to side-winds and waves. Penalty points can often be avoided in WW slalom competition with a low deck that sneaks *under* the gates.

Flat deck surfaces are more sensitive to irregular water pressure, and, in combination with edged gunwales, result in extreme sensitivity and capriciousness during leans in crosscurrents and in high waves. This responsiveness is often preferred by WW experts when paddling in complex turbulence and when executing fast Eskimo rolls.

More stability and easier handling result with oval decks and rounded gunwales, which distribute water pressure more evenly over the hull surface when ploughing, leaning and re-surfacing.

CANOES—THE BASIC MODELS

All-purpose and Touring Canoes

The standard 16-foot canoe with a beam between 36 and 38 inches and a depth of 13 to 15 inches is a good all-round model. Flat-bottomed and with minimal rocker, it offers a good compromise between buoyancy, stability, manoeuvrability and swiftness. The load capacity of 600 to 800 pounds makes it suitable for up to three paddlers plus considerable gear. It is not too long for effective control when paddling singles, and with paddlers in bow and stern (tandem) it is highly manoeuvrable. In the all-purpose and touring canoe group, the 12, 14, and 15-foot models are also common. While shorter length improves manoeuvrability, smaller load capacity and diminished swiftness are drawbacks. For carrying heavier loads on long tours over rough water, 17 and 18-foot models are often a better choice.

For touring, P-F hulls offer distinct advantages. A good 16-foot model weighs less than 50 pounds and when fitted with a *yoke* (anatomically formed carrying collar) in place of the usual *centre-thwart* (spreader), it saves drudgery on portages.

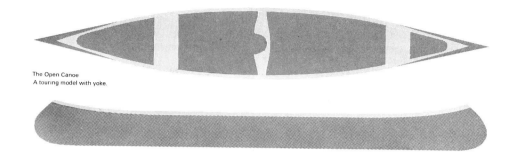

The Open Canoe
A touring model with yoke.

While most modern canoes are fitted with bow and stern seats, these are often too low for a comfortable, efficient style, or too high for good balance. Seasoned paddlers therefore prefer to use the seat as a brace for the buttocks while kneeling in the bottom of the canoe. The lowered weight increases stability and the larger base provided by knees, feet and buttocks transmits forces from paddle to hull more effectively.

Strong, waterproof, synthetic *painters* (lines) are fastened to bow and stern seats. The painters are ¼ to ⅜ inches thick and 10 to 15 feet long. They are an invaluable aid when *lining* (guiding downstream from shore) and *tracking* (guiding and towing upstream from shore) on rapids, when controlling and towing a swamped canoe, and when mooring.

Contrary to popular romantic notion, a high, upswept bow and stern do not effectively improve the seaworthiness of an open canoe in high waves. Strong side-winds make control difficult and added material increases the weight. The hull depth at its shallowest is an accurate indicator of the swamping point since it will determine the height of the gunwales above water at a given load.

When high waves and heavy spray are anticipated, a *spray deck* fastened over the gunwales is convenient. The decking must be securely attached, however, and the individual spray-skirts easily released to avoid entangling ejecting paddlers in the event of an upset.

13

White Water Canoes

The canoeist whose main interest lies in paddling on turbulent WW is best served by a specialized P-F WW canoe. In contrast to the open canoe, a permanent deck and a hull form resembling a kayak are standard.

C-1 (singles) and C-2 (doubles) models are the most common. The C-1 cockpit is located amidships; the C-2 cockpits well towards bow and stern. WW C-2s, used mainly for touring, sometimes have a large deck opening over the voluminous centre hull which facilitates loading and unloading gear. It is sealed by a spray deck en route.

Coamings recessed into the deck reduce spray (which can diminish visibility) and are less prone to damage when a capsized hull passes over shallows.

Firm positioning in the cockpit enhances control of the hull for tight manoeuvring in heavy water. At the same time, comfort and instant release for ejection are important considerations. Anatomically moulded styrofoam blocks and/or foam rubber pads affixed in the hull provide a comfortable base for kneeling. The knees are well spread for a wide base, and thigh straps or moulded supports hold them in place. The feet are braced against adjustable stem-boards underneath, and the buttocks are supported by a narrow ledge projecting forward into the cockpit from

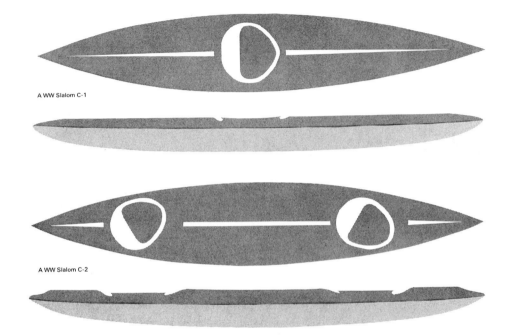

A WW Slalom C-1

A WW Slalom C-2

the coaming. Well-coordinated C-2 paddlers often angle the cockpit arrangement towards their respective paddling side for optimum stroke efficiency.

Bow and stern *grab-loops* of strong cord, recessed to hang clear of the water and reduce spray, facilitate control and recovery of a capsized hull in WW. Elastic cords, straps, or rubber clamps attached to the deck may be used to fasten a spare paddle within

easy reach. Flotation aids in bow and stern holds are mandatory.

The desirable handling qualities of WW slalom canoes in order of preference are manoeuvrability, stability and swiftness. WW racing C-1s and C-2s are designed mainly for swiftness at the price of a corresponding loss in manoeuvrability and stability. WW racing hulls are longer (5.0 m) and have minimal rocker. WW racing C-1 designs tend towards the delta-form.

The WW Slalom C-1
Competition standards:
Min. length   —   4.0   m
Beam   —   70   cm

The WW Slalom C-2
Competition standards:
Min. length   —   4.58   m
Beam   —   80   cm

The FW Racing C-1
Competition standards:
Max. length   —   5.20   m
Min. beam   —   75   cm
Min. weight   —   16   kg
The FW Racing C-2
Competition standards:
Max. length   —   6.50   m
Min. beam   —   75   cm
Min. weight   —   20   kg

Flat Water Racing Canoes

The light, fragile, delta-form FW racing C-1 and C-2 shells are an extreme specialization for speed. Designed for straight-line travel on flat water with minimum waves and wind, their practical limitations confine their use mainly to the serious competitor.

The predominantly semicircular hull is very tippy, but stability improves with lean because of the large, flat sides at the beam. Strong leans facilitate turning. The bow and stern ends are decked, forming hollow bulkheads (with drain hole and plug), and the upturned bow coaming deflects water when ploughing through waves. The stern profile is cut very low to minimize the effect of side-wind which can disadvantage a competitor when blowing from his off side (opposite the stroke side). In such a case, the bow tends to veer into the wind, requiring strong steering — and correspondingly weaker propulsive strokes — to maintain a straight course.

The paddling position is high for efficient application of propulsive strokes (but correspondingly diminished stability), the paddler kneeling on *one* knee. The moulded styrofoam / foam rubber kneeling block is fitted securely into position on floorboards which are fastened in the hull bottom. An adjustable stem-board acts as foot brace for the kneeling leg. Heel straps or an extra padded thwart hold the foot in place. This system improves balance and control for effective technique.

To be valid for international competition, FW racing canoes must comply with official design stipulations. No concave surfaces are allowed, and bow-stern profiles of the immersed hull must be mirror images from amidships. No keel or rudder is allowed.

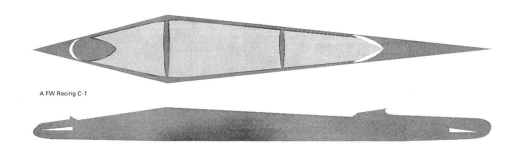

A FW Racing C-1

KAYAKS—THE BASIC MODELS

All-purpose and Touring Kayaks

A kayak between 4.30 and 4.50 m long, with a 60 cm beam, a high deck and a roomy cockpit making bow and stern holds readily accessible offers the recreational kayaker a reasonable compromise for general use and some touring. Depending on preference for speed or manoeuvrability, different combinations of design elements may be selected. The faster kayak for open waters would have a predominantly semicircular cross section, delta-form and straight keel-line including provision for a steering mechanism. A reasonably fast boat for open waters which offers better manoeuvrability on WW would have a sharp-prowed, straight-keeled, semicircular bow portion for speed and a wide, flat-oval mid-section with increasing rocker towards the stern for stability and manoeuvrability. The fusiform hull improves the craft's adaptability to different water conditions. A detachable steering mechanism adds directional stability on open stretches and can be disengaged over shallows. For touring, removable or hinged stem-board and seat facilitate stowing gear.

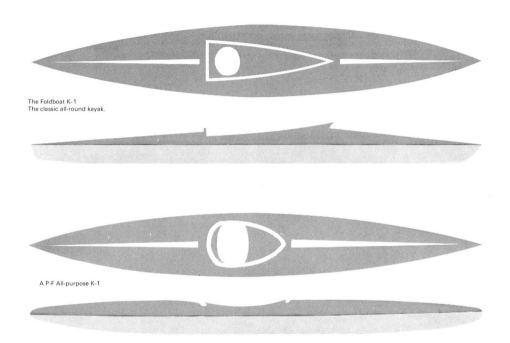

The Foldboat K-1
The classic all-round kayak.

A P-F All-purpose K-1

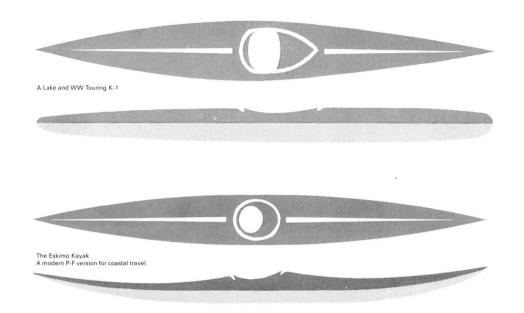

A Lake and WW Touring K-1

The Eskimo Kayak
A modern P-F version for coastal travel.

A special kayak for touring coastal waters of large lakes, seas and oceans is based on original Eskimo designs. The long (4.5 to 5.5 m) and relatively narrow (60 to 65 cm) hull sits low in the water and offers good speed and rough-water stability.

A steering mechanism maximizes directional control and the use of strong leans improves the manoeuvrability of this long craft.

The low profile reduces susceptibility to side-winds which can blow the slow-moving paddler far off course on open coastal waters.

Upswept bow and stern facilitate launching and landing in surf and paddling through high waves and breakers, and a high, ridged deck improves water run-off.

The grab-loops on all-purpose and touring and sometimes on WW kayaks are best joined by painters running from bow to stern on both sides of the cockpit. When attached by means of small snap-links, they can be quickly released for tracking and lining or controlling a capsized craft. They also provide the best hold on a swamped and slippery P-F hull.

Appropriate rubber clamps or elastic fasteners on the deck serve to hold the two halves of a spare paddle, leaving more stowage room inside for other gear.

Two-seater kayaks (K-2s) are usually enlarged versions of basic K-1 designs. They have the advantages of greater speed and larger stowage capacity. K-2s are especially useful for teaching learners under conditions above their level of ability. Their weight and length and the prerequisite of a partner, however, limit their practicality and use.

WW Kayaks

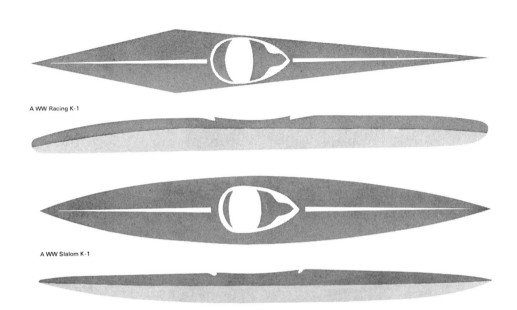

A WW Racing K-1

A WW Slalom K-1

The WW Racing K-1

Swiftness, stability and manoeuvrability is the usual order of preference of top competitors. Modern designs tend towards the extremely fast and tippy delta-form hull with semicircular / V-shaped cross section, sharp bow and stern ends and straight keel-line. The decks are high — especially the bow deck where the narrow hull requires added volume and buoyancy for plunging through waves and rollers. The wider stern deck is lower and flatter to reduce undesirable volume and veering. The delta-form is readily capsized by waves and crosscurrents catching the gunwales. Skilful WW racing competitors use leans to counteract the veering tendency and bracing techniques (which have a minimal braking effect) for balance.

The WW Slalom K-1

Slalom competition calls for maximum manoeuvrability and control in turbulent WW. The WW slalom hull is short with a flat / oval cross section, a low profile and a pronounced rocker. Fusiform shape and rounded gunwales minimize the effects of unbalanced water pressure on the deck during

The WW Racing K-1
For medium to heavy WW:

Length	—	4.50 m
Beam	—	60 cm
Weight	—	±13 kg
Ideal load	—	75 kg

The WW Slalom K-1

Length	—	4.0 to 4.20 m
Beam	—	60 cm
Weight	—	±13 kg

leans, when plunging through waves and rollers and when re-surfacing. Extremely low decks (for sneaking under gates) and the resultant edged gunwales are preferred by some slalom experts to increase hull sensitivity and thus enhance feel for the craft in heavy turbulence. Blunt bow and stern keel-lines reduce resistance to turning and are less prone to wedging between rocks.

In general, good WW slalom kayaks follow the undulations of the turbulent water surface closely and are extremely responsive.

The oval cockpit is close-fitting (40 by 70 cm) for firm seating and to reduce water pressure on the spray-skirt. A single-unit recessed coaming with anatomically moulded seat suspended 1 to 2 cm above the hull bottom is most prevalent. This system reduces jarring of the spine when passing over drop-offs or bouncing off the occasional rock. For maximum freedom of action *behind* the cockpit, the seat is best located near the middle of the cockpit with the stern deck and the coaming behind the paddler lowered slightly.

For maximum control and efficiency during strong leans, braces, tight manoeuvring and rolls, firm positioning is essential. The sides of suspended seats require structural bracing to the hull to prevent swaying in the seat during leans. Anatomically formed padded braces or knee hooks under the bow deck or projecting from the coaming, padded hip supports on the sides of the seat, supporting straps across the small of the back and properly adjusted stem-boards help to provide individualized fit for optimum comfort, ease of ejection and maximum control.

Flotation aids and recessed grab loops (with bow—stern lines) are standard equipment.

Flat Water Racing Kayaks

K-1

The long, low, **sleek delta-form** FW racing **K-1, K-2** and **K-4** are the fastest craft made for paddling. As with FW racing canoes, the extreme specialization of purpose and design limit their use to the competitive paddler.

To qualify for international competitions, official design standards must be satisfied:
No concave hull surfaces or formlines are allowed. In contrast to FW racing canoes, a steering mechanism is standard.

The streamlined delta-form with semicircular cross section exhibits the typical qualities of swiftness and directional stability acquired at the expense of buoyancy, stability and manoeuvrability. Bow volume is minimal and varies in different models, depending on the paddler's weight. The stern deck is flat, reducing the effect of side-winds to a minimum.

To allow room for the racing paddler's slightly flexed knees, the cockpit is extended forward. The recurved lip at the front of the coaming deflects waves and the coaming rim is designed for use of a spray-skirt. Although not always necessary, spray-skirts are used on choppy waters, in cold rainy weather,

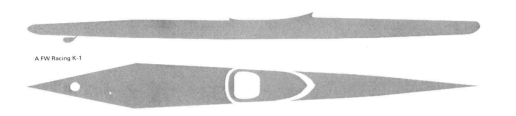

A FW Racing K-1

Class	Max. length	Min. width	Min. weight
K-1	5.20 m	51 cm	12 kg
K-2	6.50 m	55 cm	18 kg
K-4	11.0 m	60 cm	30 kg

in long distance races and when paddling in the K-2 and K-4.

A slightly raised, anatomically formed seat is fastened in the hull bottom close to the back of the cockpit, and the stem-board with steering post is located under the bow deck. Both seat and stem-board are adjustable forward and backward to compensate for leg lengths of different paddlers and to facilitate individual adjustment for the optimum stemming angle necessary for effective force transmission. In addition, weight placement forward or backward can be regulated for proper trim.

PADDLES

A good paddle is light, strong, durable and well-balanced. It should handle comfortably when paddling for long periods, and its design as well as the materials used in its construction should suit the purpose for which it is intended.

The Single-blade Paddle

Canoes are normally paddled by means of a single-blade paddle. For general use and recreational paddling, the one-piece spruce paddle is light and reasonably strong, the strength depending on the thickness of shaft and blade. A paddle made of maple, ash, black cherry, or other hardwood is stronger and more durable, but also heavier. The weight is minimized by reducing the thickness of shaft and blade. For maximum strength, one-piece paddles should have a straight, close grain running the length of the paddle.

For WW and competitive paddling, the paddle must be stronger. By combining lamina (layers) of light woods with lamina of stronger, more durable (and heavier) woods, a *laminated* paddle of considerable size and strength can be built while keeping the weight within limits. The lamina in the shaft of a well-made paddle are aligned parallel with the direction of applied stress. The neck (the part of the shaft adjacent to the blade) cross section should be oval with the longer axis also parallel to the direction of stress. The back of the blade is often reinforced with a tapering ridge-line formed by a continuation of the shaft down the middle.

A thin layer of P-F around the neck and smoothed even with the shaft adds strength and protects the wood from wear caused by levering the shaft against the gunwales when using certain steering strokes.

Unless protected by a good varnish finish, wood paddles absorb moisture, which adds weight, leads to dry-rot and causes warping. When stored for long periods, they are best suspended by the *butt* (grip) to prevent warping which can result from the weight of the paddle when it is propped up.

Durability is of special concern with paddles used mainly in WW. The blade tips are usually protected by a strip of light metal such as aluminum or by P-F. P-F blades with laminated or alloy shafts are especially suited to endure the inevitable stresses and scrapes encountered in WW paddling.

The butt should fit comfortably into the palm of the hand and provide good control for guiding and twisting the blade. A bulbous butt is most common on all-purpose paddles. The *T-grip* provides more control, and an individually fitted *formed T-grip* ensures both maximum control and comfort.

Paddle length for general use is normally between the chin and eye level of the paddler when he is standing

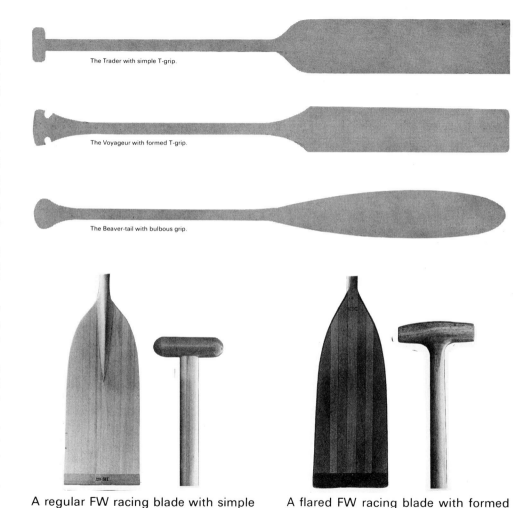

The Trader with simple T-grip.

The Voyageur with formed T-grip.

The Beaver-tail with bulbous grip.

A regular FW racing blade with simple T-grip.

A flared FW racing blade with formed T-grip.

erect, holding the paddle vertically on the ground in front of him. However, height, reach, strength, individual style and preference should also be taken into account. A more accurate method of choosing paddle length is to assume the normal paddling position in the boat and to execute a few basic strokes. If the blade is fully immersed during the power phase of the stroke and the guiding hand (on the butt) is neither too high nor too low to detract from the comfort and / or effectiveness of the style, the length is appropriate.

Blade shape and area are often selected on the basis of personal preference as well as purpose. For general use, the *beaver-tail* is common. The longer, narrower *voyageur* is suited to deep water and a high position, as in the bow. The wider *trader* is often preferred by a strong stern paddler.

The basic trader shape predominates in WW and FW racing paddles. A variation sometimes seen in FW racing blades is a flared tip. With a long reach, more blade area can be immersed at the initiation of the pull than is possible with the regular shape.

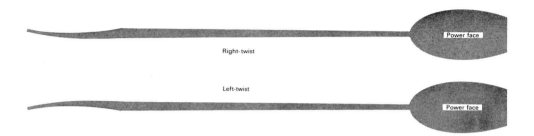

Right-twist

Left-twist

Power face

Power face

The Double-blade Paddle

The kayak is propelled by means of a double-blade paddle. As well as strength, balance and durability, *lightness* is especially important in view of its greater size. Finely crafted laminated paddles are most popular. To reduce weight, some have hollow shafts and blades of thin, but strong, multi-ply veneer. P-F blades and laminated or alloy shafts are often used for WW paddling.

Double-blade paddles are available in a separable version. The two halves are joined by means of a light metal *ferrule* (sleeve) and held in place by a small screw. A separable paddle has the advantage of easy storage and transport. As a spare paddle on tours, it can be stored inside the hull or fastened to the deck. The ferrule joint is, however, a potential weak spot and adds weight.

The blades of a kayak paddle are always *feathered* (set at right angles to each other). The advantage is that as one blade is immersed for the stroke, the upper, recovering blade slices through wind and spray with minimum resistance. Depending on which hand aligns the blades for each stroke, the paddle is either *right-* or *left-twist*. The twist is especially significant with curved blades, where the concave (hollow) side is always used as the *power face*. Natural inclination and individual preference usually determine the twist chosen. Right-handed paddlers tend to prefer the right-twist and left-handers the left-twist.

To improve shaft strength and also provide a better feel for blade alignment, the shaft cross section near the blades should be oval, with the long axis parallel to the line of applied stress.

The blade shape may be symmetrical and square-tipped or asymmetrical and oval-tipped. The power face may be flat, concave, or spoon-shaped. Spoon blades usually have a sharp centre-ridge to minimize side-slip during the pull.

Flat blades are advantageous for the inexperienced paddler (especially in WW) when learning complex manoeuvring strokes with alternate forward and backward paddling. The lack of permanent twist is advantageous when the paddle must be used by a group (e.g., club or family) with different twist preferences.

Curved blades are designed to concentrate the pulling force in the middle of the power face so that maximum power will be maintained throughout the stroke. Concave / square-tipped and spoon / oval-tipped blades are characteristic of FW racing paddles. WW paddles are predominantly concave / square-tipped, but with less curvature than FW racing paddles to reduce undesirable side effects during quick manoeuvring and when using slicing strokes in turbulent waters.

Blade area is usually determined by the amount of *slip,* if any, desired during the pull. Strong paddlers prefer a large blade for minimal slip; others compensate for small blade area with a high stroke rate.

Reach, strength, style and purpose influence the choice of paddle length. WW paddles tend to be short for quick stroking; FW paddles long for extra reach. In team K-2s and especially K-4s

Symmetrical, Concave / Square-tipped Blades

— laminated
— laminated, with protector strip for WW

Asymmetrical, Spoon / Oval-tipped Blades

— veneer, men's FW racing
— laminated, women's FW racing

the stroke (bow paddler who sets the stroke rate) normally uses a short paddle, while each successive paddler has a slightly longer paddle because the hull gradually widens in the delta-form. In choosing a paddle of the proper length, the paddler must consider the width of the hull at the paddler's position, and that the blade area must be fully immersed for optimum efficiency of propulsion.

For general reference:
Touring   — ± 220 cm
FW racing   — ± 220 cm
WW slalom — 210 to 215 cm
WW racing — 215 to 220 cm

Chapter 2   Canoeing and Kayaking Technique

FUNDAMENTALS

Single-blade and Double-blade

Single-blade technique is asymmetric; the skilful canoeist paddles on one side only, either left or right. By means of strokes with a *pry* component, directional control on the opposite side is maintained. In situations where especially effective or strong control is required, the paddle is *crossed* over, but without changing grip.

Most paddlers have a preferred paddling side, but canoeists should try to develop their off side for balanced exercise and versatility. On extended tours, for instance, *switching* (crossing and changing grip) every half day or so is desirable. However, switching in order to maintain direction or execute a turn involves a break in stroke rhythm and a balance shift, and a moment of non-control occurs as the hands change grip. Here, switching usually indicates lack of control and is obviated by good single-blade technique.

Double-blade technique is symmetric, with alternate application of strokes on both sides of the kayak. Directional control is achieved by maintaining or changing, as required, the balance of forces between the left and the right side. Since no change in grip is neces-sary, a rhythmic, balanced and highly efficient style is characteristic of good double-blade technique.

When paddling two, three, or more to a boat, the bow paddler *always* sets the stroke rate and the others follow his rhythm. In this way, maximum pro-pulsive force and efficiency are ob-tained as all blades simultaneously apply equal force in the same direction (straight-line travel). In canoes, ''left'' and ''right'' paddlers are distributed appropriately so that the forces on both sides balance. In kayaks, the crew apply strokes simultaneously on the *same* side. As well as contributing to total propulsive force, the stern paddler in a team canoe is responsible for hold-ing course and general manoeuvring on flat water. For abrupt direction changes on FW and especially in WW (where better overview in the bow makes recognition of the best passage easier), the bow paddler initiates the steering action and the stern comple-ments appropriately. For this reason, the more experienced paddler usually assumes the stern position on FW and the bow position in WW. In team kayaks, experience in *pacing* (setting the stroke rhythm) and race *tactics* (for distance events especially) are more valuable in the bow where the steering mechanism is also operated.

Holding the Paddle

In general, the hands are spaced so that the elbows form right angles when the shaft of the paddle is held horizon-tally on top of the head. When paddling ''left,'' the left hand grasps the neck of the single-blade paddle, and the butt is held in the palm of the right hand. The left arm pushes / pulls in the ap-propriate direction; the right hand con-trols blade angle by twisting the butt to maintain an effective blade angle throughout the stroke. When paddling ''right,'' the hands are reversed.

With a right-twist double-blade paddle, the right hand grasps the right neck firmly with the power face of the right blade angled as for a basic stroke on the right. The wrist is straight. The left hand grasps the left neck loosely, allowing the shaft to rotate in the hand. The grip of the right (twist) hand is maintained, and the feathered left blade is aligned for the next stroke by flicking the back of the right wrist up (hyperextension). With a left-twist paddle, the roles of the hands are reversed. During the stroke, the twist (top) hand controls and maintains the blade angle while the bottom hand transmits the main stroke force.

It is important to remember that the paddle should never be squeezed tightly, and that the hand should be relaxed during *recovery* (the non-active phase of the stroke). Excessive muscular tension is avoided during the power phase by pushing / pulling with straight wrist. The curved fingers transmit pulling forces and, with a double-blade, the crotch formed by the thumb and the index finger transmits pushing forces.

Embarking and Disembarking

Hilarious, if not unpleasant, situations in the paddling sports usually arise when the unsuspecting novice or unthinking expert first steps into a tippy canoe or impossibly cramped cockpit. Briefly reflecting on the concepts of balance and hull stability *before* making that first step will often prevent an unexpected dunking.

Launching: the hull is rested on the thighs and slid hand-over-hand into the water.

To get into an open canoe:
1. The hull is brought as close as possible to the embarkation point (shore).
2. The paddle is positioned for left or right paddling and is laid across both gunwales for a *paddle brace*. The paddler holds the shaft and the gunwales with his hands.

3. The foot is placed *over* the keel-line in the hull. The weight is transferred smoothly from shore to the foot in the hull, keeping the weight low by flexing the knees. Light, even pressure on the hands maintains balance as the shore leg is brought in and the foot placed next to the foot over the keel-line.
4. A kneeling position is assumed, keeping weight low and centred. The singles paddler now slides into position next to the gunwale on his paddling side, his buttocks resting on his heels and his toes pointing back.

In *trimmed* team canoes, the paddlers assume their positions over the keel-line one at a time and then shift simultaneously on the stern's command. In untrimmed canoes, the paddlers shift one at a time; the others are prepared to brace. Then final weight and load shifts are made for proper trim.

To get into a cockpit:
1. First, put on the spray-skirt and roll up the hem.
2. The paddle is placed from shore to the rear coaming for the paddle brace.
3. The outside hand grasps the paddle shaft and the coaming *over* the keel-line, and the inside hand grasps the shaft on the shore side *near* the coaming.

4. The outside leg is placed into the cockpit, and the weight is transferred smoothly from shore to the hands on the shaft — the hand over the keel-line supporting most of the weight.

5. The other leg is brought into the cockpit, and the weight is lowered into the seat over the keel-line.
6. The paddle is brought forward and rested on the coaming. To fasten the spray-skirt, first hook in at the back, then at the front. Finish with the sides while holding down the front.

To disembark, these procedures are followed in reverse, remembering to keep weight low and over the keel-line. In team boats, *one* paddler disembarks at a time.

Ejecting

Before the roll is mastered, and often after, *ejecting* from the cockpit of a closed hull is a frequent procedure. To eject from a close-fitting cockpit:
1. Stay calm; orient yourself; hold on to the paddle.
2. With one hand, pull on the release loop (tab) of the spray-skirt hem in front, releasing the hem from the coaming.
3. Lean forward, relax the legs, and push yourself *back* and *out*, clearing the rear coaming with the buttocks.
4. Upon re-surfacing, hold on to a grab-loop and swim to shore, keeping the hull upside-down to prevent shipping water.

Emptying

On shore, a swamped hull is best emptied by two persons, but a lone paddler can prop up one end and work with the other.

1. *Never* attempt to lift a swamped hull directly on to shore. The weight will not only strain the back but can also break the hull.
2. Tilt the boat on its side and lift slowly, allowing the water to drain from the hull (through the cockpit).
3. Residual water is drained from the decked hull by turning the hull upside-down and alternately raising and lowering one end with respect to the propped-up end.
4. When no props are available, a decked hull may be *levered* upside-down over one knee. The empty, higher end forms a long lever arm which can be lowered slowly to raise the short end and drain the water.
5. In shallow water, a partially swamped decked hull may be emptied by pressing one end down (the cockpit is up) so that the water collects in the lower end, and then rotating the hull (the cockpit is turned down) and lifting up (the cockpit is above water) to allow the water to drain through the cockpit. If water still remains, the hull is rotated again (the cockpit is turned up), the end lowered, and so on until the hull is emptied.

PADDLING DYNAMICS

A skilful paddler applies appropriate strokes automatically, with a minimum of conscious analysis. However, when first learning to paddle an unfamiliar craft or paddling in untested waters, an understanding of the fundamental forces involved and their effects on the craft can help to solve problems, correct mistakes and polish technique.

Paddling involves forces which affect the *speed* and *direction* of the hull relative to the water. These forces are continually acting between the water and a floating hull, and, during the stroke, between the water and blade and the paddle and hull.

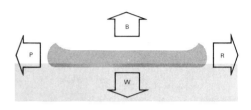

Water:Hull

In order for the craft to float, the buoyant force (B), which equals the weight of water displaced by the hull, must equal the downward force of the weight (W) of hull + load. When W exceeds B, the hull sinks. Since the more voluminous the hull, the more water it can displace and the more buoyant the craft will be, allowing it to carry heavier loads.

For the hull to continue moving or to accelerate relative to the water, the propulsive force (P) must be respectively equal to or greater than the resistance (R). Propulsive force is generated by the paddling action; resistance by the friction between hull and water and by wind. Maximum paddling efficiency is attained by maximizing P and minimizing R.

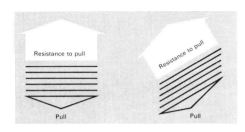

Water:Blade

Water resists efforts to pull or push the flat blade through it. In fact, it is the tendency of the blade to momentarily "stick" in the water which allows the paddler to push or pull the hull *around the paddle* during the stroke.

Maximum resistance and therefore maximum propulsion is generated (a) when the blade's power face is held at right angles to the direction of pull, (b) when the area of the immersed power face is large, and (c) when the pull is long and powerful.

The resistance is directed *diagonally* to the direction of pull when the blade is held at an angle.

Paddle:Hull

Firm positioning in the hull allows the paddler to effectively push or pull the hull around the paddle sticking in the water. The reaction of the hull depends on the radius (distance) of the immersed blade from the hull's pivot point (usually the centre of gravity) and the direction of the push or pull relative to the hull's centre-line.

Strokes applied close to the pivot point and parallel to the centre-line have minimal turning effect and are most efficient for straight-line travel.

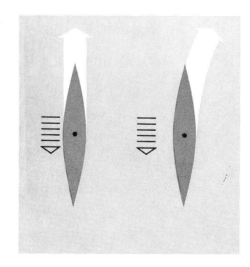

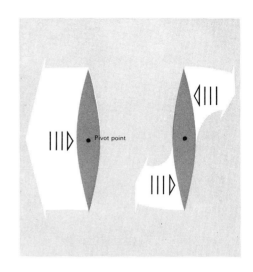

Strokes applied far out from the pivot point and at right angles to the centre-line have maximal turning effect.

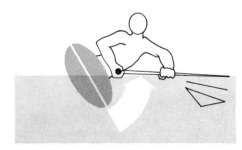

Vertical strokes applied far out from the pivot point and at right angles to the centre-line have maximal rotational (rolling) effect.

STROKE MECHANICS

Theory of paddling dynamics and analysis of stroke mechanics can reinforce — but never replace — practice and experience gained on the water. Smooth, efficient paddling technique results from a continuous blending of stroke elements. Blade angle, radius, direction of applied force and power are fused for optimal effect in a given situation. The skilful paddler feels the requirements of the hull of which he is an integral part. In most instances, his responses are instinctive, reflex manipulations of the paddle.

Strokes, therefore, should not be viewed as rigid conjoinings of basic stroke elements. For analysis, however, this separation can hasten the novice's learning process — provided the end result is kept in view. For the expert, analysis may give insight leading to refinement and perfection of technique.

The Basic Stroke

The basic stroke is for forward (or backward when executed in reverse) propulsion.

The blade entry is made as far forward as comfortably possible by extending the pulling arm and rotating torso and shoulder forward. The blade is immersed as vertically as is comfortable and held at right angles to the direction of pull.

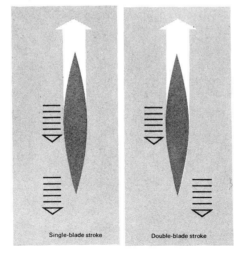

Single-blade stroke   Double-blade stroke

The blade should be immersed completely before the main pulling force is initiated.

The pull is directed backward, parallel to the centre-line and as close to the gunwale as possible.

Pulling arm and wrist are straight, the power emanating from torso rotation.

The upper arm complements the pull with some straightening, the hand being pushed forward at eye level. The shaft is kept vertical.

The pull is terminated at hip level. The upper hand is dropped and the recovery initiated by *slicing* the blade sideways and up out of the water.

The blade is swung forward for the next stroke with the paddle held horizontally and the blade angled to slice into the wind. Arms should be relaxed and loosely extended as torso and shoulder are rotated forward again for the entry.

A unique variation of the normal single-blade recovery is the silent, underwater recovery of the "Indian" stroke in which the blade is sliced smoothly forward through the water and remains submerged for the entire stroke cycle.

A continuous Indian stroke requires that the paddle be revolved 180 degrees with each stroke cycle: 90 degrees at the end of the pull (power face *out*) and 90 degrees at the beginning of the subsequent pull (power face now faces forward and the "back" of the blade becomes the new power face).

With a double-blade, the dropping of the upper hand is accompanied by simultaneous forearm flexion of the lower arm. The blades are thus aligned automatically for the next stroke.

STRAIGHT-LINE TRAVEL

Since the basic stroke is executed at a radius from the pivot point (radius depending on hull width), each stroke tends to turn the bow away from the stroke side. The symmetric double-blade style results in straight-line travel when stroke forces on both sides are *balanced*. The asymmetric single-blade style, however, requires a lateral pry component to offset this turning effect. Since most hulls tend to veer — once the bow begins to turn, the stern slides out and forward, quickly pivoting the hull — the pry is best applied at the stern to offset veer and keep the hull aligned. Under normal conditions, the pitch stroke, the J-stroke, and the Canadian stroke are the most efficient for straight-line single-blade travel. In heavy WW where quick *bracing* (leaning on the paddle to improve balance or prevent upset) may be necessary, the stern pry (unfortunately often called the *goon* stroke) is preferable.

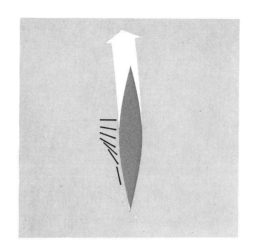

The Pitch Stroke

1. The propulsive component is applied as with the basic stroke. The hull pivots and the bow swings away from the stroke side.
2. The steering component is applied in the latter half of the stroke. The butt is twisted to angle the blade's power face away from the centre-line as the pull continues.

The dynamic pry effect (created as pull is exerted on the *angled* blade) is best transmitted to the hull by sliding the shaft along the gunwale. Applied *behind* the pivot point, the pry forces the stern away from the stroke side, pivoting the hull for realignment.

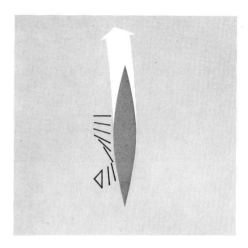

The J-stroke

A stronger pry effect is attained by using the J-stroke.

1. The propulsive component is applied as with the basic stroke. The hull pivots, and the bow swings away from the stroke side.
2. The blade is angled at hip level as for the pitch stroke, and the pull continues.
3. As the blade passes the hip, and the power face faces away from the centre-line, the top hand pulls the butt horizontally across towards the centre-line. The shaft is levered against the gunwale resulting in a strong pry effect, forcing the stern away from the stroke side and pivoting the hull for re-alignment.

In both pitch stroke and J-stroke, the power face is angled away from the centre-line by twisting the butt so that the thumb of the hand points forward at the end of the twist.

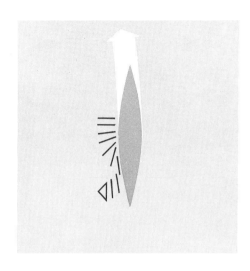

The Canadian Stroke

Simpler to execute but requiring more "feel" for paddle control, the Canadian stroke is often preferred by skilful paddlers for straight-line travel.

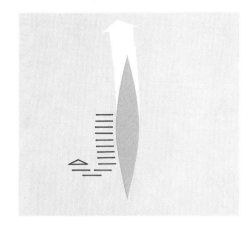

The Stern Pry

The stern pry is best suited for straight-line travel in turbulent WW.
1. The propulsive component is applied as with the basic stroke. The hull pivots and the bow swings away from the stroke side.
2. At hip level, the butt is twisted to angle the power face toward the centre-line.
3. As the blade passes the hip, and the back of the blade faces away from the centre-line, the top hand pulls the butt horizontally across towards the centre-line. The shaft is levered against the gunwale, pry-ing the stern away from the stroke side and pivoting the hull for re-alignment.

In contrast to the pitch stroke and J-stroke, the power face is angled towards the centre-line by twisting the butt so that the thumb of the hand points back towards the paddler at the end of the twist. This hand position allows instant application of a brace as the blade is recovered or, more importantly, at any time during the stroke. (The hand position at the end of the pitch stroke and J-stroke is awkward and must first be reversed before an effective brace is possible.)

1. The propulsive component is applied as with the basic stroke. The hull pivots and the bow swings away from the stroke side.
2. Slightly behind hip level, the blade is sliced sideways up, forward and out of the water by dropping the butt hand as the lower hand stabilizes.
3. As the blade is sliced up and forward in the water, the blade angle is adjusted and stabilized for more or less resistance (at the non-power face) as required.

This resistance (drag) applied at a distance from the pivot point pivots the hull, pulling the bow towards the stroke side for re-alignment.

The lack of a strong paddle twist and pry component results in a natural hand position throughout the stroke and allows a paddler to maintain a high stroke rate comfortably without sacrificing efficiency.

The blade is in good position for instant bracing at any time during the stroke.

TURNS

A turn results when an unbalanced force is applied on one side of the hull. In single-blade paddling, repeated basic strokes without a pry component turn the bow away from the stroke side. Repeated pitch, J-, stern pry and Canadian strokes with a very strong steering component at the stern turn the bow towards the stroke side. In double-blade paddling, a repeated or more powerful basic stroke on one side will turn the bow away from the stroke side.

The more effective turning strokes and techniques initiate a turn by forcing the bow into the new direction and enhance the stern slide appropriately.

Leans

A lean increases rocker and alters the shape of the water line around the hull, rounding it on the lean side and straightening it on the other. When the hull is moving forward in the water, water pressure at the bow is increased on the more rounded lean side and reduced on the straighter side. This unbalanced force turns the bow away from the lean side.

When the paddler is firmly positioned in the cockpit of the canoe or kayak, a strong lean is executed by flexing sideways at the hips while keeping the

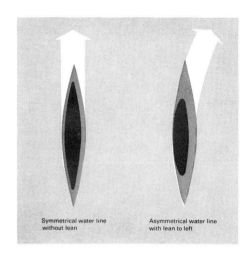

Symmetrical water line without lean

Asymmetrical water line with lean to left

upper body vertically balanced. When paddling singles in an unloaded open canoe, a most effective permanent lean is achieved by assuming a low kneeling position adjacent to the gunwale on the paddling side. The tilted hull also brings the paddler closer to the water, facilitating good style and effective control.

Unweighting

By bending forward or backward at the waist, the stern or bow end respectively may be unweighted. In a turn, the unweighted end of the hull slides out more easily, facilitating the turn.

By using appropriate leans and unweighting, the singles paddler can greatly enhance the turning effect of repeated or unbalanced basic strokes as well as many of the special turning strokes.

Sweeps

Sweeps can be used whether the boat is stationary or moving and the turn is facilitated by a lean to the stroke side and unweighting.

The Bow Sweep

The Bow Sweep

Also called the front sweep, this stroke is used to turn the bow *away* from the stroke side.

The blade is immersed as far in front of the pivot point and as close to the hull as is comfortable. The blade is angled vertically and the power face faces out.

The sweep is directed outward and back in a wide, flat arc. The first half of the sweep forces the bow away from the stroke side.

The sweep is continued and the blade is recovered by slicing up and out of the water *before* meeting the hull. The latter half of the sweep pulls the stern towards the stroke side, continuing the pivot.

Depending on the degree of pivoting desired, the singles paddler may sweep fully from bow to stern or he may shorten the arc. In a C-2, the bow sweep is used mainly by the bow paddler, the first half of the sweep being most effective.

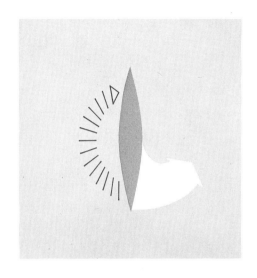

The blade is immersed as far behind the pivot point and as close to the hull as is comfortable. The blade is angled vertically and the back of the blade faces out. A backward lean unweights the bow, and reversing the grip on the shaft (single-blade only) facilitates the sweep action.

The Stern Sweep

Also called the reverse sweep, this stroke is used to turn the bow *towards* the stroke side.

The sweep is directed outward and forward in a wide, flat arc. The first half of the sweep pushes the stern away from the stroke side, pivoting the hull and swinging the bow towards the stroke side.

The latter half of the sweep pulls the bow towards the stroke side, continuing the pivot. When the craft is moving forward, this sweep causes a strong braking effect.

Depending on the degree of pivoting and braking desired, the singles paddler may sweep fully from stern to bow or he may shorten the arc. In a C-2, the stern sweep is used mainly by the stern paddler, the first half of the sweep being most effective.

Cuts

Cuts are only effective when the hull is *moving* relative to the water.

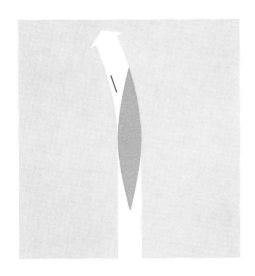

The Bow Cut

The blade is immersed vertically as far in front of the paddler as is comfortable and well out from the centre-line. The power face faces in, and the *leading* edge of the blade is angled out in the new direction.

The paddle is stabilized in this attitude for the duration of the cut. Leaning forward towards the blade increases reach and unweights the stern, enhancing the turn.

The dynamic action of water flowing against the angled power face tends to deflect the blade away from the hull. By stabilizing the paddle, the bow is pulled to the stroke side, pivoting the hull.

The Stern Cut

Applied behind the pivot point by assuming a backward lean and using the same blade angle as for the bow cut, the stern cut pulls the stern towards the stroke side, pivoting the hull and swinging the bow *away* from the stroke side.

Bow Cut and Stern Cut

Cross-bow Cut and Stern Cut

Cross-bow Cut and Stern Pry

The Cross-bow Cut (single-blade only)

This stroke is often used to advantage in the bow of a C-2 and in a WW C-1 to turn the bow strongly away from the normal stroke side.

Without changing grip, the paddle

is swung low and horizontally across the hull in front. Then the paddle is stabilized in the appropriate bow cut position.

Some single-blade paddlers stabilize the paddle by clamping the shaft against the gunwale with the lower

hand. Although this transmits the turning forces more directly to the hull, the attendant rigidity of this technique can upset balance and / or diminish adaptability and responsiveness of style.

Rudders (single-blade only)

Often called running pries, rudders depend on the dynamic action of water flowing against the stabilized, angled blade. In contrast to cuts, rudders tend to push the hull away from the stroke side.

The Bow Rudder

The blade is immersed as far as is comfortable in front of the pivot point.

The normal power face is placed flat against the contour of the hull and the paddle is stabilized at an appropriate angle.

The dynamic action of water flowing against the angled blade deflects the blade against the hull, prying the bow away from the stroke side.

The pry effect may be increased by twisting the butt to lever the *trailing* edge of the blade out.

A stylish one-handed version of the bow rudder is achieved by sliding the lower hand up to the butt to become the control hand and slicing the blade smoothly forward into rudder position well ahead of the pivot point.

Bow Rudder and Stern Rudder

The Stern Rudder

Applied behind the pivot point, a stern rudder prys the stern away from the stroke side, pivoting the hull and swinging the bow *towards* the stroke side.

39

Cross-bow Rudder and Stern Cut

The Cross-bow Rudder

The paddle is swung low and horizontally across the hull in front, and the blade is stabilized in rudder position against the hull *without* changing grip. The bow is pried towards the normal stroke side.

The usefulness of the cross-bow rudder is limited since a bow cut on the normal stroke side has the same effect without necessitating crossing over.

Because of the *direct* transmission of forces from blade to hull, rudders can be highly effective. However, the strong prying and turning effects (especially in the bow) require practice and concentration for balance and control.

LATERAL TRANSLATION

Lateral translation is characterized by broadside (sideways) transpositioning of the hull with no turning — the hull alignment before and after the stroke is parallel. It is useful for approaching or moving away from landings. In WW, lateral translation allows obstructions to be dodged without changing hull alignment relative to the current.

Any stroke which generates forces acting at right angles to the centre-line causes lateral translation when applied *beside* the pivot point or, in a team boat, when simultaneous balanced strokes are applied by the paddlers, so that the net effect acts at right angles to the centre-line and through the pivot point.

Draw, pry and sculling strokes are especially effective for lateral translation in any water, whether the boat is stationary or moving. Applied ahead of or behind the pivot point, they are also highly effective as turning strokes.

Draws

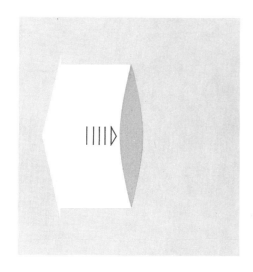

The blade is immersed vertically and as far out from the gunwale beside the pivot point as is comfortable.
The power face faces in and the blade is angled parallel to the centre-line.

The pull is directed in a straight line towards the gunwale and at right angles to the centre-line.
The hull is ''drawn'' towards the blade.

A bow draw applied ahead of the pivot point draws the bow towards the stroke side.
A stern draw applied behind the pivot point draws the stern towards the stroke side, pivoting the hull and swinging the bow away from the stroke side.

To avoid undesirable levering, the recovery is initiated *before* the paddle meets the gunwale. The butt is twisted through 90 degrees and the blade is sliced outward for the next draw. (Alternatively, the blade may be sliced back and out of the water.)

Bow Draw and Stern Draw

Cross-bow Draw and Stern Draw

Pries (single-blade only)

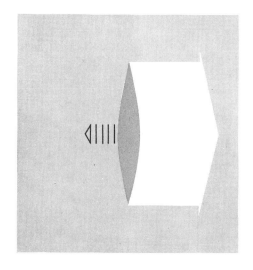

The cross-bow draw (single-blade only) is used effectively in the bow of a C-2 and often in a WW C-1.

Without changing grip, the paddle is swung low and horizontally across the hull in front and into positon for the draw. The bow is pulled strongly away from the normal stroke side.

A bow pry applied ahead of the pivot point pushes the bow away from the stroke side.

A stern pry applied behind the pivot point pushes the stern away from the stroke side, pivoting the hull and swinging the bow towards the stroke side.

The blade is immersed directly beside the pivot point, adjacent to the gunwale and slightly underneath the hull. It is angled parallel to the centre line and the back of the blade faces out.

The upper hand pulls the butt across towards the centre-line and at right angles to it. Simultaneously, the lower hand pushes the shaft away from the centre-line and at right angles to it. The hull is pried away from the blade. An efficient variation is to lever the shaft against the gunwale for the pry. Here it is important to keep the pulling arc on the butt short to avoid prying the gunwale down and upsetting the balance.

The butt is twisted through 90 degrees and the blade is sliced back to the starting position for the next pry.

Bow Draw and Stern Pry

Skilled canoeists often pry with *one* hand only (on the butt) and, by levering the shaft on either gunwale, prevent broadside drifting when the canoe is stationary.

Quick, repeated prying at bow or stern make the pry very useful for correcting hull alignment in WW. In the C-1, it is often the quickest (although a cross-bow draw is more efficient) stroke for minor lateral translation away from the stroke side.

43

Sculling

Sculling strokes depend on the dynamic action of water deflecting the *angled* blade as it is moved through the water. Blade angle and the direction of pull or push determine the effect on the hull.

Sculling strokes are especially useful when continuous force (and thus control) must be applied.

The Sculling Draw

This stroke allows application of a continuous draw. Applied at bow and stern, the effect is identical to bow and stern draws.

The blade is immersed at a comfortable distance out from the gunwale and ahead of the pivot point. The power face faces in and the back edge of the blade is angled out.

The angled blade is pulled back parallel to the centre-line, to a comfortable distance behind the pivot point. The dynamic effect of water on the angled blade tends to deflect the blade out from the centre-line, and the hull is drawn towards the stroke side.

The butt is twisted so that the front edge of the blade is angled out.

The angled blade is now pulled forward, parallel to the centre-line and back to the starting point. Again, the blade is deflected out, and the hull is drawn towards the stroke side.

The angle is reset for the backward pull, and so on.

The Sculling Pry

By reversing the angles used for the sculling draw, a continuous pry can be applied for lateral translation away from the stroke side. Applied at bow and stern, the effect is identical to bow and stern prys.

For effective force transmission, the shaft is sometimes slid along the gunwale during the sculling action.

COMBINED STROKES

Combined strokes reflect the ability of the skilful paddler to fuse elements of different basic strokes into one smooth, contiguous stroke which best meets the hull's momentary requirements.

The S-stroke

Here, the strong turning effects of a bow cut and bow draw are combined with a sculling draw and finally a stern draw to achieve lateral translation with a minimum loss of forward speed. The S-stroke is especially useful for avoiding obstacles in WW racing.

The C-stroke (single-blade only)

This stroke combines the strong turning effect of a bow draw with the propulsion and aligning forces of a J-stroke.
It is useful for negotiating strong turns *towards* the stroke side while maintaining good forward speed and for a single paddler who is attempting straight-line travel in an open canoe while a broadside wind is blowing from the stroke side.
The strong bow draw and stern pry counteract the tendency of the wind to blow the bow away from the stroke side, while the propulsive element maintains forward speed.

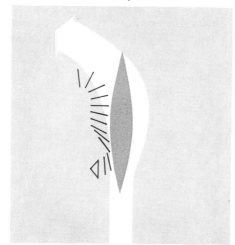

The Figure 8-stroke

The strong draw effects of bow and stern draws are combined with the continuous draw effect of a sculling draw. When executed beside the pivot point with balanced bow and stern "loops," the figure 8-stroke results in a strong lateral translation to the stroke side. When one loop is stronger (larger, with more powerful draw), lateral translation and simultaneous pivoting of the hull result. By reversing stroke direction, a continuous, strong pry effect is achieved.
The figure 8-stroke is useful where precise control of hull alignment during

draws or pries is necessary, and when a strong continuous draw or pry effect is desired.

The Circle-stroke

This stroke combines the turning effects of a bow draw and a stern pry to pivot the hull. A bow pry and a stern draw pivot the hull in the opposite direction.

The circle-stroke is especially useful when a quick pivot is required or when a singles canoeist must turn a long hull on-the-spot in a confined space.

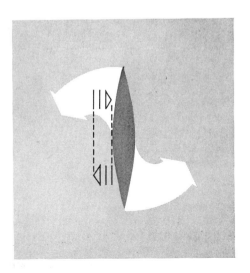

BRACING

Unbalanced vertical forces acting at a distance from the centre-line and at right angles to it cause the hull to *rotate* (roll) on its long axis. Bracing involves balancing the rotational forces acting on the hull — usually to keep it from capsizing.

Most strokes have some rotational component which has a bracing effect. The specialized braces have a very strong rotational effect which enhances stability in heavy WW, allows quick recovery from a near-capsize and, in the case of Eskimo rolling, efficient righting of a capsized hull.

In essence, braces allow the paddler to transfer some or most of his weight to the paddle, allowing the hull to be easily turned, leaned, or righted by appropriate hip action.

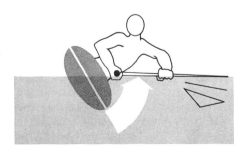

The Flat Brace

The paddle is extended horizontally out to the side and at right angles to the centre-line. The back of the blade faces down.

The paddler braces by leaning on the shaft and stabilizing (or pulling up) with the other hand. Simultaneous lateral hip flexion rights the hull underneath.

Flat braces are most effective when the blade is at the *surface* and pressure on the shaft is discontinued as the blade is pushed under. The blade is sliced up and out for recovery.

Quick and easy to apply, flat braces are very effective for recovery from a near upset and for stabilizing the craft in turbulent WW.

on the angled power face, the more the weight which can be transferred to the paddle and the more extreme the lean can be.

The recovery is initated by a strong draw towards the hull with simultaneous lateral hip flexion to right the hull underneath.

The high brace is usually applied ahead of the pivot point, and it pulls the bow strongly to the stroke side. Simultaneously, the stern slides out and forward to enhance the pivot.

The Low Brace

The low brace is essentially a flat brace applied behind the pivot point and combined with a stern sweep action.

The brace allows extreme unweighting of the stern and execution of a strong lean to the stroke side for increased rocker, facilitating turns to the stroke side. To be effective, high initial speed into the turn is required. The stern sweep action tends to slow the hull down.

In WW, the low brace is often used for turns into oncoming currents when extra stability is desired.

The High Brace

Also called the Duffek stroke (after the Czech originator), the high brace is a "hanging" stroke which facilitates extreme leans, balance being maintained by literally hanging on the stabilized paddle. To be effective, the high brace requires high relative velocity of water flow against the angled blade. It is therefore most useful in WW. On FW, the hull must be moving forward at high speed.

The blade is immersed and stabilized as for the bow cut. The upper hand is high (top of the head) and controls the blade angle relative to flow direction for optimum bracing effect. The greater the dynamic action of the water

The Sculling Brace

This is a more dynamic version of the flat brace and offers a continuous bracing effect.

The paddle is extended out to the side with the back of the blade facing down. The blade is swept back and forth in a comfortable arc with the leading edge angled up. The dynamic action of water on the angled blade tends to deflect the paddle up during the sweeps. This allows weight to be transferred to the blade for the brace as the control hand stabilizes and twists the shaft for appropriate blade angle.

The sculling brace is useful for practising controlled leans and determining the capsizing point of a hull. During

embarking and disembarking of paddlers, a sculling brace adds stability. It is most useful to keep a tippy FW racing shell upright when stationary.

A high sculling brace has the same effect as a sculling draw. The bracing component allows application of a strong, continuous lean to facilitate the draw.

ESKIMO ROLLING

The rigours of Arctic climate demanded an effective method of righting a capsized kayak without shipping water or having to swim for shore. Having designed an ingenious craft, the inventive Eskimos provided an equally ingenious solution — the Eskimo roll.

Although the roll may appear to be the capstone of paddling technique, its original survival value clearly indicates that it is a *fundamental* skill and should be learned early. Indeed, rolling can save much time and effort otherwise expended in swimming to shore and emptying the craft before paddling can be resumed — time and effort better used for perfection of paddling techniques.

Except for a re-orientation required when hanging upside-down from the capsized hull, rolls — when executed properly — demand no more strength and skill than a strong brace. In essence, the roll is a flat sculling brace executed from under the hull.

A decked hull, a waterproof spray-skirt, and firm positioning in the cockpit are basic requirements for successful rolling. Before attempting a roll, the paddler should have sufficient experience to eject comfortably when necessary. When first learning to roll, it is best to practise in shallow water where an experienced paddler can stand to help the roll when necessary and correct weak points in technique. For these sessions, nose plugs increase comfort and a face mask improves the view, facilitating orientation.

Note: In using the illustrations to practise the following rolling techniques, hold the paddle, as is demonstrated, in the upright position, brace the knees against the kneehooks by pressing the heels down, sweep the blade back to the starting position and fall in on the *sweep* side. After orienting, begin the sculling sweep as demonstrated, keeping the following points in mind:

1. The leading edge of the blade is angled up as for the sculling brace so that the blade is deflected up to the surface during the sweep.
2. The blade is swept in a wide, flat arc until the paddle is at right angles to the centre-line.
3. The start of the sculling sweep allows pull to be directed downward on the shaft. *At this moment,* lateral hip flexion is initiated to rotate the hull back under the paddler.
4. As the sweep continues, the upper body is pulled to the surface and the hip flexion rights the hull under the paddler.

5. As the paddle comes to right angles with the centre-line, a final downward push as for the flat brace allows the upper body to be lifted out of the water for completion of the roll.

Fast rolling is facilitated when the starting position for the sweep can be assumed *before* capsizing. Also, it is generally more efficient to roll through (fall in on one side and roll up on the other). In currents, it is easier to roll up on the downstream side. When properly executed, rolls can be used in less than 3 feet of water.

For versatility, rolls should be perfected in a variety of water conditions, on both sides, and without a pre-assumed starting position. In preparation for WW, rolls practised with a partly swamped or loaded (touring) hull give valuable experience.

The Cross-grip Roll

The long lever arm and the more natural upright position of head and torso under the capsized hull make the cross-grip roll easy to use and highly efficient under most conditions. When capsizing unexpectedly, the hand *opposite* the falling side crosses (changes) grip from the shaft to the blade. It controls blade angle as the other hand sweeps the blade forward as for a stern sweep with a sculling brace angle. The cross-grip roll normally rolls the paddler up on the same side to which he capsized.

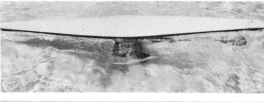

◀ The Short Roll

This is the most-used roll, particularly in WW where fast rolls without a change in grip are advantageous.

The roll is facilitated by leaning well forward on to the bow deck for the start of the sweep and quickly changing to a strong backward lean during the sweep.

The control hand is lifted high out of the water to clear the hull with the non-active blade at the start of the sweep.

The Long Roll ▶

This variation of the short roll affords a longer lever arm creating a stronger rotational force on the hull and facilitating the roll. The problem of clearing the hull with the non-active blade is avoided, and control of the sculling angle is easier.

The long roll is sometimes used as an intermediary step to learning the short roll.

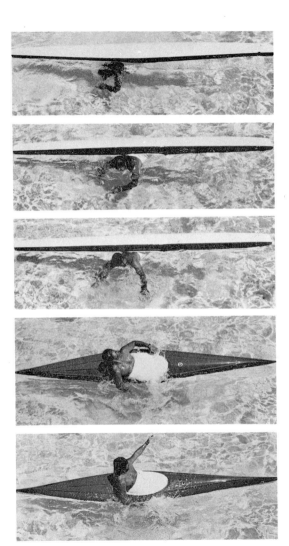

The Roll "Sans Paddle"

This roll offers the ultimate in fail-safe recovery — even in the event of a lost or broken paddle.

The roll is facilitated by first shifting the body position farther forward into the hull until the coaming is under the armpits.

A sculling *breast-stroke* action brings the upper body to the surface as lateral hip flexion initiates hull rotation.

A final strong downward stroke is executed as the outside arm is simultaneously flung horizontally across to the other side.

By keeping the head and torso well back on the stern deck, the paddler accumulates sufficient rotational momentum to right the hull.

The short lever arm of this roll limits its usefulness to FW and occasionally to WW with ideal current and minimal turbulence.

Rolling a Canoe

The higher paddling position in a canoe requires more leverage to bring the upper body out of the water. The shorter single-blade paddle, however, provides less leverage during the sculling and flat brace action. Especially early and strong lateral hip flexion are therefore necessary to rotate the hull.

Often the paddle will sink too deep during the final flat brace. A quick recovery slice to the surface followed by another flat brace is then necessary to complete the roll.

Short and cross-grip (with shaft hand reversed as for the stern sweep) rolls are most effective for rolling canoes.

When rolling a WW C-2 or a K-2, the sweeps are executed *simultaneously* on the *same* side, requiring one paddler to switch sides. Short or cross-grip rolls are suitable, and the start of the sweep is indicated by a predetermined knocking signal on the hull.

Chapter 3   White Water

White water can offer the ultimate challenge and the most enjoyment to the paddler who has mastered complete control of his craft on flat water. To propel, manoeuvre and stabilize his craft on WW, the skilful paddler coordinates boat alignment and stroke action with the dynamic action of currents flowing in different directions at different velocities.

Quick recognition of flow patterns and split-second response with paddle and hull are prerequisites for effective WW technique.

For the WW competitor, paddling strength and endurance, perfection of WW tactics, and psychological preparedness ensure good performance.

WW DYNAMICS

The flow of water in natural streams and rivers is characteristically turbulent. Changes in the course of a stream-bed and obstructions in the stream-bed divert the moving water, causing a separation of flow and the formation of eddy (rotating) currents in the region of discontinuity of flow. The higher the *flow velocity* and the more abrupt the *diversion,* the greater the degree of resultant turbulence. For instance, a flow velocity of 5 m / sec in an unobstructed channel

may be navigable whereas the same velocity in an obstructed channel may cause dangerously excessive turbulence.

Flow Velocity

Flow velocity depends on the *gradient* (steepness) and *morphology* (shape) of the stream-bed as well as the *volume* (quantity) of water carried.

Gradient

In heavily obstructed passages, a gradient of 2% (i.e., a drop of 2 feet over a distance of 100 feet) approaches the upper limit for safe paddling.

Morphology

Due to friction, flow velocity is least along the bottom and sides, and maximum just below the surface over the *deepest* part of the stream-bed.

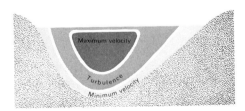

An abrupt *narrowing* of the stream-bed (e.g., a chute) reduces flow velocity and

raises the *head* (water level and pressure) as the water backs up in front of the narrows. The rise in head increases flow velocity through the narrows. Conversely, an abrupt *widening* causes a drop in head and reduces flow velocity.

Volume

During spring run-off or floods and after heavy rains or cloudbursts, flow volume increases dramatically. The resultant head in turn increases flow velocity. Since one cubic metre of water weighs one metric ton, the forces generated at high flow volume are considerable.

In general, the easiest and safest passage is found where flow velocity is highest — over the deepest and least obstructed part of the stream-bed. It is characterized by the smoothest flow or the highest, most regular wave formations.

Flow Patterns

Meanders, obstructions, drop-offs and crosscurrents create a variety of recognizable flow patterns. The skilful WW paddler is an expert at assessing flow patterns and using some of their characteristics advantageously during manoeuvres, while avoiding others.

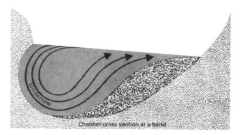

Channel cross section at a bend

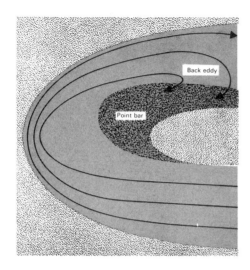

Back eddy

Point bar

Meanders. Bends in a stream-bed divert the *entire* flow volume, creating correspondingly powerful flow patterns. *Centrifugal force* causes water flow to converge on the outside bank, with a corresponding reduction of flow on the inside. The resultant separation of flow forms a *back-eddy* (rotating current with *upstream* flow) on the inside bank.

The accumulation of water on the outside bank raises the head. The increased pressure forms a vertical eddy with strong undertow adjacent to the outside bank and boils and up-wellings towards the inside.

Because of the differing flow rates at the opposite banks of a meander, erosion occurs at the outside bank where the water is flowing quickly, and the eroded material is deposited by slow moving water on the inside bank forming shallows and point bars. On fast-flowing streams, a high outside bank may be *undercut*.

The fastest and safest course around a bend is usually along the outside bank. However, unexpectedly smooth water adjacent to a vertical outside bank often indicates an undercut. To avoid being swept against the wall by centrifugal force, choose a course closer to the inside bank. If capsized and forced against the wall, dive deep, swimming *with* the undertow of the vertical eddy.

The *shear zone* (zone of interaction) between mainstream and back-eddy currents is characterized by *irregular turbulence* — small eddies, holes, boils and up-wellings. It is best avoided or crossed quickly.

Obstructions. Obstructions may be visible or submerged. They are characterized by the formation of an hydraulic jump or pillow (abrupt rise in water level) on the upstream side and a back-eddy on the downstream side.

Behind boulders, trees, pylons, bridge abutments and similar obstructions in the mainstream, a characteristic white, foaming "V" with apex directed *upstream* is formed, which indicates the shear zone between the mainstream and the back-eddy currents. Depending on the size and shape of the obstruction, high velocity and volume of flow create strong, extensive back-eddies with *souse holes* (depressions) and *rollers* (vertical eddies) directly behind the obstacle, followed by *standing waves* (permanent wave formation), and/or haystacks and *breakers* (very high standing waves with white caps) downstream.

The best route through obstructed ▶ channels is indicated by the dark tongue of the mainstream current flowing between the white, foaming shear zones of adjacent obstacles. Approaching from upstream, the mainstream tongue often resembles a dark "V" with the apex directed *downstream*.

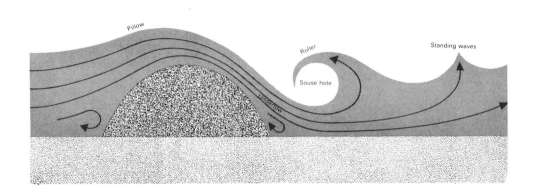

Pillow

Roller

Standing waves

Souse hole

Undertow

If the hull broadsides against an obstruction, always lean *downstream* towards the obstruction. The lean exposes more hull surface to the direction of flow which often causes the hull to be lifted over or around the obstacle. Leaning upstream exposes gunwale and deck to the current and invites quick upset. If capsized, avoid being trapped between the obstacle and broadsided hull!

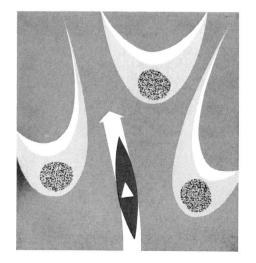

If the water is *aerated* (foamy) as it flows over a submerged obstruction, it is usually too shallow to avoid scraping the hull.

Submerged or floating trees, roots and branches are an especially dangerous form of obstruction which should be assiduously avoided by appropriate evasion manoeuvres well upstream. Minimal diversion and deceleration of flow are caused by this type of obstruction, the effect being similar to water straining through a sieve. The hull is easily capsized and held against the obstacle by the powerful current. If collision appears unavoidable, it is often best to eject and climb up on the branches before capsizing, keeping the boat aligned parallel to the current and hauling it up and over.

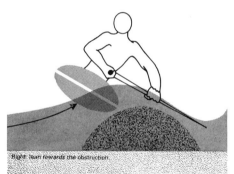

Right: lean *towards* the obstruction.

Wrong: leaning upstream invites upset.

Drop-offs. Ledges, falls, dams, weirs, spillways and chutes involve an abrupt drop in height over a short distance. The flow is diverted downward, velocity is increased and powerful undertows and rollers are created. Drop-offs are characterized by an *hydraulic drop* (abrupt drop in water level) upstream of the brink. The water is usually aerated as it falls and a powerful, aerated roller is formed at the foot of the fall. A foaming back-eddy is followed by high standing waves.

Avoid rollers with a strong upstream eddy current. They can stop a boat and throw it continually back into the roller, trapping the paddler.

Rollers are best crossed at right angles and at high speed.

If allowed to broadside, the hull is quickly stopped and held.

The foamy water provides little support, but a *deep* downstream brace will sometimes find sufficient support to pull the hull free of the roller.

If capsizing appears imminent, it is best to fall in on the downstream side where the water is deeper.

If capsized and forced to eject, dive deep and swim downstream following the current of the undertow.

Crosscurrents. Irregular turbulence occurs in the shear zone between currents flowing in different directions and/or at different velocities.

The shear zone of currents moving parallel but in opposite directions is characterized by eddies and whirlpools whereas a white, foaming roller is formed at the shear zone of currents colliding at an angle and sliding over/under each other.

Currents flowing from the stream-bed to the surface form boils and up-wellings. Currents flowing down from the surface form holes and undertows.

The interaction of high waves creates areas of relative calm when the wave periods are *out of phase* (crests meet troughs). Conversely, extremely high waves and deep troughs result when the wave periods are *in phase* (crests meet crests).

In general, shear zones of irregular turbulence are best avoided or crossed quickly but carefully, the paddler taking their action on hull and paddle into consideration. On the other hand, shear zones and irregular turbulence often provide valuable information about the currents which the seasoned WW paddler incorporates into his manoeuvres.

GRADING WW

A standardized assessment of the difficulties posed by specific WW stretches is an invaluable aid to recreational and touring paddlers as well as the WW enthusiast. Used properly, WW classification can help the paddler decide whether his skill and equipment are appropriate for the challenge. On maps and river guides, it can help avoid unpleasant and sometimes dangerous surprises on a tour. For the WW competitor, it serves as a measuring stick of competence which is useful for training and improving technique.

Since WW conditions are affected not only by stream-bed characteristics but also by flow volume, fluctuations in water level can easily render a WW classification useless. It must be remembered, therefore, that *average* flow volumes are normally used for permanent classification. Good river guides also classify for maximum and minimum water levels. On tours, the time of year and attendant periods of flood and drought in the area must be taken into consideration. Under all circumstances, unfamiliar WW is best reconnoitered first on foot.

Unobstructed Flat Water

Suitable for all types of craft.

FW A : Standing water or water flowing at less than 0.5 m/sec.

FW B : Water flowing between 0.5 and 1.0 m/sec which can be overcome by back-paddling.

FW C : Water flowing faster than 1.0 m/sec which cannot be overcome by back-paddling; launching and landing require care; some manoeuvring skill is required for bends and back-eddies and to avoid simple obstacles.

Obstructed WW

WW I Easy:

Occasional rapids characterized by low, regular waves.
The best passage is easily recognized.
Obstructions (boulders, sandbars, trees, etc.) are easy to avoid.
Suitable for open canoes (OC), foldboats (F-1 & F-2), WW kayaks (K-1 & K-2) and canoes (C-1 & C-2).
Spray cover is not necessary.

WW II Medium to Difficult:

Frequent rapids characterized by high, regular waves.
Easy to medium drop-offs (chutes, ledges, falls).
Back-eddies and shear zones are easily negotiated.
The best passage is generally easy to recognize.
Suitable for OC, F-1 & F-2, K-1 & K-2, C-1 & C-2.
Spray cover may be helpful.

WW III Difficult:

Numerous rapids with high and irregular waves, breakers, rollers and back-eddies.
Difficult drop-offs.
Suitable for F-1 & F-2, K-1 & K-2, C-1 & C-2.
Upper limit for OC.
Spray-skirt necessary.

WW IV Very Difficult:

Long rapids characterized by high and irregular waves, breakers, powerful back-eddies, whirlpools and sharp bends.
Drop-offs with powerful rollers and undertow. (Drop-offs above WW IV are generally not passable.)

Best passage often difficult to recognize. Reconnoitering advisable before attempting unfamiliar stretches.
Suitable for F-1, K-1 & K-2, C-1 & C-2.
Spray-skirt mandatory, as well as helmet, life-vest and flotation aids in the hull.

WW V Exceedingly Difficult:

Long, continuous rapids with very high and irregular waves, breakers, haystacks and powerful rollers which cannot be avoided.
Extremely fast currents with powerful whirlpools and boiling back-eddies.
Reconnoitering mandatory.
Suitable for K-1 and C-2.
Spray-skirt, helmet, life-vest and flotation aids mandatory. Eskimo roll compulsory.

WW VI Extreme:

All WW V difficulties intensified to the upper limit of present-day skill and equipment.
Passable under ideal conditions only.
Suitable for K-1 and C-2.
All safety equipment compulsory.
Safety personnel should be stationed on shore, ready to assist.
In general, WW IV is a good test of skill for advanced WW paddlers. WW V and WW VI are for the most experienced and accomplished WW athletes only.

WW ACCESSORIES

Intricate manoeuvring of sensitive WW craft in complex and powerful currents often leads to capsizing. Although capsizing and rolling are not the aim and purpose of WW paddling, they do form an integral part of the modern WW sport. For safety reasons, appropriate equipment is therefore *compulsory*.

The Spray-skirt. Good spray-skirts completely seal the hull to water. An effective seal around the coaming and a snug — but not binding — fit around the waist are mandatory. Elastic suspenders are sometimes used to keep the waistband in position during vigorous paddling action, when passing through high waves and rollers, and when Eskimo rolling and swimming in fast WW. The release tab should be handy to allow quick ejection.

The best spray-skirts in use today are made of neoprene and are designed to form a taut, flat cover for the cockpit. A high, broad waistband ensures good fit and added warmth around the sensitive kidney area.

The Cockpit Sack. A waterproof cockpit sack is especially advantageous to the paddler when training on WW before the Eskimo roll has been mastered. Fastened over the coaming and lining the cockpit area, the sack effectively seals the rest of the hull to water. With repeated capsizing and ejection, little water is shipped so that the hull may be emptied quickly and easily.

The Helmet. Capsizing in obstructed WW calls for suitable head protection. Good WW helmets are made of lightweight, durable, waterproof synthetics. Adequate dampening space, sides projecting down to protect the temple area, perforations which provide adequate ventilation and allow quick draining of water, and a secure, comfortable fit are prime considerations. Hockey helmets are sometimes used.

The Life-vest. No paddler should venture into WW without a life-vest. A fit which allows free movement for the paddling action, a buoyant force of at least 20 pounds and a design which buoys up the *front* of the chest are desirable qualities. A good life-vest facilitates rolling, improves overview when swimming in WW, offers added insulation in cold water and makes rescue by companions easier in the event of unconsciousness.

The Wet-suit. Under cold WW conditions of spring floods and glacier-fed mountain streams often encountered by the serious WW paddler, a diver's neoprene wet-suit immeasurably improves comfort and safety. Cooling rapidly causes stiffening of joints, weakening of muscles, loss of coordination and eventually, loss of consciousness. A ⅛ to ⅜ inch thick wet-suit can increase the retention of body warmth ten- to twelve-fold. Paddlers generally prefer ⅛ inch neoprene, as thicker material tends to bind and restrict paddling action.

For maximum freedom of action, WW competitors often wear only the wet-suit pants, preferring a light, waterproof shell to the more binding neoprene jacket. However, the pants alone should only be worn in combination with a life-vest to prevent the face being forced into the water when swimming.

Footwear. Running shoes protect the feet when walking or swimming in shallow WW and provide reasonable grip and support when portaging. High-laced shoes are less likely to be pulled off in fast currents, and quick-drying material improves comfort.

WW TACTICS

Good WW tactics reflect the paddler's ability to maximize or minimize the dynamic effect of currents flowing against hull and blade. The effect is minimal when blade and hull are angled *parallel* to direction of flow. It is maximum when blade and hull are at *right angles* to flow direction. When held at an angle relative to flow direction, blade and hull are deflected laterally.

A mastery of paddling technique, quick recognition of current patterns and correct assessment of their effects on blade and hull facilitate precise, decisive and smooth manoeuvring in turbulent WW.

Basic WW tactics are best practised downstream of small chutes or spillways where there are well-defined back-eddies on both sides, standing waves not more than 3 feet high and calmer waters with accessible banks farther downstream. More time is available for training if the Eskimo roll has been learned beforehand.

Launching in a Current

If possible, choose a location where
—the water is easily accessible,
—the water is calm or flowing slowly parallel to shore,
—the water is flowing upstream (i.e., a back-eddy).

The hull is aligned parallel to flow direction (shore) with the bow pointing upstream for a *bow-first entry* or the stern pointing upstream for a *stern-first entry* into the mainstream.

1. While embarking, keep the hull aligned parallel to flow direction.
2. Use the paddle bridge for stability. Do not let go of the paddle. If the current is too strong and tends to sweep the craft away or turn it broadside, look for a more suitable launching site.
3. Fasten the spray-skirt. Hold on to the paddle!
4. Use the paddle to push off, or apply a draw to pull the hull away from shore.

Entering the Mainstream Current

Bow-first Entry Into Mainstream

1. Paddle upstream with the back-eddy and angle the bow slightly into the mainstream.
2. As the bow cuts into the mainstream, apply a brace with a lean downstream. The parallel but opposite currents swing the bow downstream and the stern upstream. The hull pivots easily around the stabilized paddle.
3. Apply the first few propulsive strokes carefully — especially on the upstream side — until the hull is aligned parallel to mainstream flow.

Using a High Brace

Using a High Brace

Note spare paddle fastened to deck

Using a Low Brace

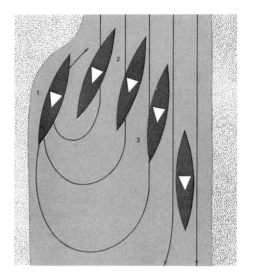

Stern-first Entry Into Mainstream

1. Back-paddle upstream with the back-eddy.
2. When the hull is adjacent to the shear zone, apply a stern draw to pull the stern into the mainstream.
3. Align the craft parallel to the mainstream flow with a few back-paddling strokes. If a strong mainstream current threatens to sweep the stern downstream, broadsiding the hull, counteract with a strong bow sweep on the shore side.

Requiring minimal leaning and involving no abrupt pivoting, the stern-first entry is especially suited for use when paddling an *open canoe*.

Exiting the Mainstream Current

Bow-first Entry Into a Back-eddy — The Eddy-turn

The eddy-turn is a highly effective method of stopping the boat when travelling downstream at high speed.

1. Approach close to the shear zone and point the bow at a slight angle into the upstream flow of the back-eddy.
2. Apply a high brace so that the blade catches the full force of the back-eddy current.
3. Lean strongly towards the stabilized paddle, but control the lean to counteract the tendency of the mainstream current to roll the upstream stern gunwale under. The parallel but opposite currents swing the bow upstream and the stern downstream. The hull pivots quickly around the stabilized paddle and comes to a dead stop.

The smallest back-eddies in the midst of a rushing torrent are suitable for the eddy-turn, which provides a safe and efficient method of checking downriver progress. The paddler has time to rest momentarily, reconnoiter the next section and re-position his craft advantageously for the passage to the next back-eddy. The spectacular hanging strokes used for the eddy-turn are the trademark of modern WW technique.

At *slower* speeds, a strong bow sweep may be used to turn the bow into the back-eddy. As the bow enters, lean to expose the hull bottom to the upstream flow of the back-eddy. Similarly, a low brace may be used to turn the bow into the back-eddy. The brace is applied in the back-eddy current to prevent the mainstream current from catching the blade and rolling the upstream gunwale under.

Stern-first Entry Into a Back-eddy

1. Align the hull early enough to allow a *close* approach adjacent to the back-eddy.
2. Apply a stern draw to pull the stern into the back-eddy.
3. Back-paddle to keep the hull aligned and to stop the boat in the back-eddy.

The stern-first entry is useful when no change in downstream alignment is desired. The absence of strong leans and quick pivoting make it an advantageous technique when paddling an *open canoe.*

Crossing Fast Currents

In WW, it is often necessary either to cross the mainstream current from one shore to the other or to cross currents from one back-eddy to another (eddy-hopping) with a minimum of *downriver displacement.* Ferrying allows lateral translation in a strong current to align the craft with the most suitable passage, to avoid obstructions and to manoeuvre towards a better landing site.

Ferrying

To counteract the downstream flow, the hull is aligned parallel to direction of flow and the paddler paddles "upstream", against the current.

When the bow is pointing downstream and the flow velocity is *less* than 1 m/sec, normal back-paddling is sufficient to prevent downriver displacement.

However, when the flow velocity is *greater* than 1 m/sec, back-paddling is usually insufficient. It is better to swing the bow upstream (in a back-eddy) and to apply strong propulsive strokes to prevent downriver displacement.

By setting the hull on the *upstream* slope of a standing wave, the boat tends to "slide" upstream. *Sliding* is an effective technique to counteract downstream flow when ferrying across strong currents.

To achieve lateral displacement, the upstream end of the hull is angled slightly towards the side of intended displacement.

The dynamic effect of water flowing against the angled hull deflects it laterally across the current.

If the angle between hull and flow direction is too large, the boat broadsides and is swept downstream.

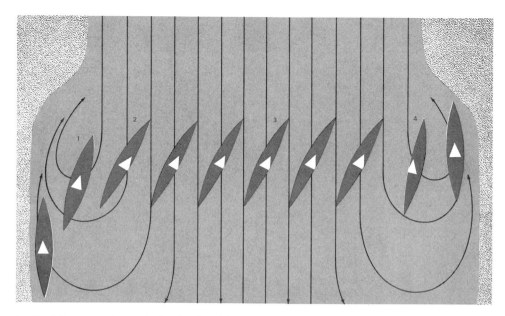

1. Paddle strongly with the back-eddy flow to increase upstream momentum.
2. Point the bow into the mainstream (at a slight angle) and lean downstream appropriately.
3. Continue paddling strongly upstream to counteract mainstream flow, and adjust strokes to maintain the hull angle relative to flow direction.
4. As the craft enters the other back-eddy, switch to an upstream lean to prevent the back-eddy current from catching the downstream gunwale and rolling the boat.

Sliding *upstream* on a standing wave

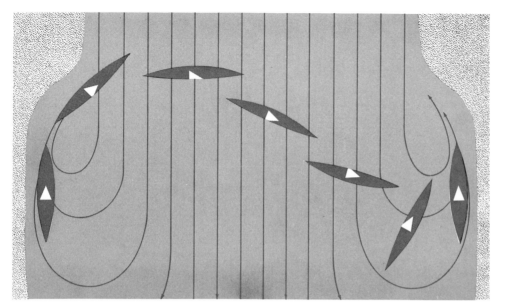

Auxiliary Loops

When negotiating obstructed passages with ferrying techniques or when the bow unintentionally crosses the shear zone into a back-eddy, the force of the mainstream may swing the hull broadside. Unless counteracted immediately, complete broadsiding is difficult to avoid.

Often it is best to let the hull swing through 180 degrees and to continue the section in *reverse* (i.e., bow pointing upstream). The craft may be reverted to the previous alignment (i.e., bow pointing downstream) by

—ferrying to the next back-eddy and applying a bow sweep or bow draw to force the bow into the back-eddy and then re-entering the mainstream bow-first,

—allowing the stern to enter (carefully) a back-eddy so that the currents pivot the hull through 180 degrees again,

—using bow sweeps on the up-stream side and stern sweeps on the downstream side (or a bow draw and a stern pry with a single-blade) to pivot the hull through 180 degrees.

A 360 degree auxiliary loop (an eddy-turn followed by a bow-first entry into the mainstream) is often a safe and efficient method of re-aligning for a difficult section downstream.

Crossing

A quick, spectacular method of crossing strong, narrow currents from one back-eddy to another is to combine a *high-speed* bow-first entry into the mainstream with an eddy-turn into the back-eddy.

When paddling upstream in the back-eddy for a bow-first entry into the mainstream, unweight the bow with a backward lean. Otherwise the bow may nose into the undertow upstream of the roller, which can drive the bow under and sometimes capsize the craft.

For fun, skilled paddlers sometimes purposely combine this strong under-tow effect with the upstream flow of the back-eddy to execute an "end-over-end" roll.

Negotiating Bends

In addition to the effect of the mainstream flow, centrifugal force causes the hull to slide towards the outside bank in a fast bend.

Setting. Setting uses the principles of ferrying and is desirable when a powerful current demands care and precision to avoid the craft's being swept against the outside bank.

Back-paddling reduces speed relative to downstream flow as the upstream stern end is angled towards the inside. Since the currents in a bend are not always parallel to shore, back-paddling and angling must always be directed *relative to flow direction.*

▼

Cutting-the-corner. Bends are negotiated at higher speeds by angling the bow sharply towards the inside bank and using strong propulsive strokes. The best route for cutting a corner is usually adjacent to and along the shear zone between mainstream and back-eddy.

If downriver speed is not all-important (as it is in WW racing competition), an eddy-turn behind the bend may be used to finish off the turn.

▼

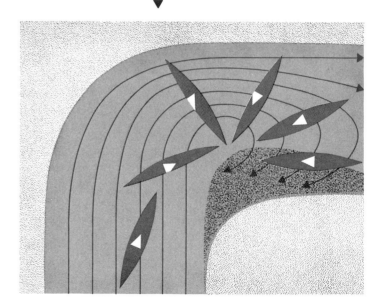

Standing Waves, Breakers, Haystacks

The tendency of the hull to slide sideways off these WW formations is minimized by maintaining good downstream speed relative to the current, using a *symmetrical* end-on or broadside approach and by applying braces as required.

Eskimo Rolling in WW

In addition to mastering basic rolling techniques, the skilful WW paddler can sometimes use currents to advantage or alter his technique for a given situation. To prepare for the various possibilities encountered in WW, the paddler should practise:
— falling in on the upstream side and rolling up on the downstream side. The current *increases* stroke effectiveness.
— falling in on the downstream side and rolling up on the upstream side. The current *diminishes* stroke effectiveness.
— falling in on one side and up on the *same* side.
— rolling in shear zones, standing waves and rollers. Turbulence and insufficient support in foaming waters diminish stroke effectiveness.
— rolling a craft loaded with gear and / or partly filled with water. (More powerful stroke and hip action are necessary to initiate the roll.)

Landings

One of the most important skills in WW paddling is the ability to make a controlled landing where and when necessary. Constant foresight, quick decisions and appropriate tactics executed with good technique are prerequisites.

Constantly scan ahead for back-eddies (to halt downriver progress) and suitable landing sites (e.g., accessible bank, slow current parallel to shore).

Take advantage of back-eddies, currents and wave formations for turning and ferrying the craft into position for the landing.

Initiate the manoeuvre far enough upstream (e.g., aligning for an eddy-turn) to avoid missing the landing.

If a good landing site has been missed, turn off into the next back-eddy and try to work upstream by ferrying and eddy-hopping.

When approaching unfamiliar stretches, try to land well *upstream* of the last landing site. This allows for a possible "miss" and also gives the following crews time and opportunity to make a landing.

Tracking and Lining

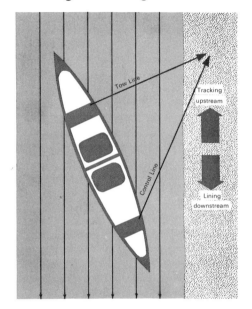

Impassable or shallow rapids can often be passed by tracking and lining, which obviates the necessity of portaging boat and equipment — an advantage with heavily laden touring craft. The technique is similar to ferrying.

By pulling on the downstream painter, the upstream end of the hull is angled slightly out into the current. The current deflects the hull away from shore.

Appropriate tension on the upstream painter allows the hull to be tracked upstream or lined downstream as the paddler walks along the shore.

If the hull tends to broadside out from shore, *relax* tension on the downstream painter.

If the hull tends to broadside in towards shore, *increase* tension on the downstream painter.

Note: When tracking and lining open canoes, the painters are best fastened to the bow and stern seats in the form of *halters*. One end is secured to the offshore side of the seat, the line brought under the hull and looped once around the shore side of the seat. An appropriate non-slipping, non-jamming knot such as the bowline is used to secure the painter at water level.

The halter method minimizes the rotational forces acting on the hull when painters are simply tied to the higher bow and stern decks or gunwales.

In strong currents, an open canoe is best tracked and lined with stern facing upstream. Attached at seat level, the stern painter offers better control since it is closer to the upstream end of the hull.

Depending on the shoreline and the obstructions encountered, 50-foot painters may be required.

Bow / stern seat or thwart

Bow-line is tied at water level

Painter

The halter for tracking and lining an open canoe

WW SAFETY

Safety Measures

Before setting out on unfamiliar rivers or streams:

Collect as much information as possible about the water to be encountered from river guides, large-scale topographic maps, local inhabitants and other paddlers who have paddled the stretch. Take note of gradient, locations and grades of rapids, locations of drop-offs (falls, dams, chutes) and gorges as well as the best portage route around them. Also take into consideration the water level which can be expected during the time of the outing.

Check that all equipment (boats, flotation aids, grab-loops, painters, paddles, spray covers, wet-suits [if necessary], helmets and life-vests) are in good condition. Repair or replace defective items.

Include special safety equipment such as a spare paddle, a throw-rope with a weighted end and a first-aid kit.

Assess the swimming and paddling expertise of all participants and stay clear of WW which exceeds their competence.

Don't travel alone! Groups of 3 to 5 boats with at least two experienced crews are ideal. The pace is always dictated by the weakest crew. For larger groups, split up into subgroups of 3 and leave plenty of space between each subgroup.

Arrange to use a system of *visual* signals (the roar of WW often drowns out shouts) to indicate danger ahead, a better passage, a landing and, in the event of an upset, that all is well.

Every member of the group should be trained to render basic first-aid (especially artificial respiration).

Once on the water:

Before entering unfamiliar sections, land well upstream and scout ahead on foot. If possible, stay at water level as heights tend to render high waves and difficult drop-offs harmless-looking. To assess complex turbulent flow patterns and to gauge re-surfacing times from under rollers and undertows, throw a piece of wood into the water upstream of the obstruction and observe its progress through the passage.

Stay alert for unmarked and unexpected rapids or drop-offs. Wind and steep or heavily forested banks can muffle the roar of falling water. Flat, slow-flowing water with a pronounced line of demarcation (hydraulic drop) in the distance usually indicates a dam, weir, chute or spillway. A white mist hanging above indicates a steep drop-off or falls.

Always proceed in single file with sufficient distance between boats to allow free manoeuvring and time to check downriver progress. The best crew enters the section first and tries to establish the best passage and tactic. The second-best crew follows last and acts as a safety check for the weaker crews between. Visual signals transmit necessary information to upstream crews.

If a landing becomes necessary, land well upstream of the last suitable site to give following crews a chance to select and manoeuvre towards a site.

If a dangerous — but passable — section lies ahead, send one man downstream to the difficult spot on foot and with a throw-rope.

If too late or badly positioned for a compulsory landing, eject (keeping the hull upright) and climb up on the nearest obstruction, while holding on to the paddle and the grab-loop.

If capsized and unable to roll up on the second attempt, eject rather than risk injury by drifting upside-down over obstructed passages.

After ejecting from a capsized craft, *always* leave the hull upside-down. The trapped air increases the buoyancy and makes the hull useful as a swimming aid on less obstructed waters.

In heavily obstructed WW, it is often better to abandon a capsized hull for the sake of personal safety.

Capsizing is part of the fun and challenge of WW paddling. Be prepared!

Rescue Techniques

Self-rescue and Swimming in WW

WW paddlers must be good swimmers able to cover long stretches underwater with their eyes open. A life-vest is mandatory and, in cold waters, a neoprene wet-suit is standard equipment. Once capsizing appears imminent, take a deep breath. Once under the hull, bend at the waist to increase clearance between head and stream-bed.

After ejecting:

Leave the hull upside-down, grasp a grab-loop and let the hull swing downstream so that it lies parallel to flow direction.

Don't become trapped between the broadsiding hull and an obstruction.

Stay on your back and keep your legs downstream and in front for protection.

In shallow rapids, try to stand up and stride quickly to shore keeping knees high.

In deeper rapids, try to push off from the bottom and use this "hopping" technique to work towards shore.

Try to use currents to advantage. By swimming "upstream" and angling towards shore, the paddler can "ferry" to shore.

It is usually easier to land on the outside bank of a bend, but the strong current makes the landing rough.

Dive through rollers head-first, keeping the arms straight in front for protection.

Pucker the lips to prevent inhalation of water spray and take deep breaths before diving.

In deep flat water, it is often possible to right a capsized decked hull by quickly depressing one end and spinning the hull so that minimal water is shipped. To get back into the boat, straddle the stern deck and, keeping weight low by bending forward at the waist, slide forward to over the cockpit. Drop the seat in first and resume the paddling position.

Assistance from Another Boat

In turbulent WW, it is most difficult to render effective assistance from another boat. On flat water, an abandoned paddle may be grasped parallel with the rescuer's paddle and a capsized hull which has not shipped too much water can often be nudged to shore.

Assistance from Shore — the Throw-rope

The throw-rope offers an excellent method of assisting a stranded or a swimming paddler in difficult WW. A strong, lightweight rope of durable, waterproof synthetic material is weighted at one end with a buoyant object (e.g., a plastic bottle partly filled with water), and a sling is tied in each end.

A safety-man with a throw-rope may be posted downstream of a difficult section *before* it is attempted by other paddlers. In the event of an unexpected upset, the rescuer can paddle quickly downstream of the capsized paddler, land and assume a ready position for the throw.

The throw-rope must be kept neatly laid together and stowed in a handy location in the boat. *Practice* ensures throwing accuracy.

To assist a *stranded* paddler, the rope is thrown across and *upstream*. The current carries the rope within his reach.

To assist a *swimming* paddler, the rope is thrown across and slightly *downstream*. The current carries the swimmer faster than the rope, allowing him to catch up.

The swimmer can hold on to the sling, or, if he is exhausted and the opportunity exists, he can tie the rope around his chest under his armpits.

The swimmer is pulled across and guided downstream with the current. Never pull against the current! The force of the current can cause the rope to be torn loose from the paddler's grip.

If the swimmer is caught in a roller, pull across along the length of the roller, not downstream where the powerful back-eddy current can tear him loose.

WW COMPETITION

WW competition introduces the elements of time and a prescribed route to provide a competitive challenge in testing the technical skills and the physical prowess of the WW paddler. At higher levels of competition, top physical condition and finesse in WW tactics are characteristic of the successful WW competitor.

WW Racing

WW racing is the distance event of WW competition. The aim is to cover the downriver distance between the start and the finish in the shortest time. The distance is usually determined by the length of uninterrupted WW III stretch available. A minimum distance of 3 km or a maximum total time of 45 minutes are the usual prerequisites. In international WW racing competition, the events are the men's K-1, C-1 and C-2. Paddling endurance, stamina, technique and good tactics are important assets for WW racing.

WW Slalom

WW slalom is probably the most spectacular paddling competition. *Gates* suspended over the water mark a prescribed course which is designed to pose every imaginable WW problem. The course must be covered in the shortest possible time while passing correctly through the gates to minimize the accumulation of *penalty points*. Expert paddling technique and perfection of WW tactics are necessary to manoeuvre the craft over the sinuous course. Paddling strength, stamina and psychological preparedness are additional assets.

WW Racing Tactics

Trial runs and / or reconnoitering the course are important. Time is reduced by choosing passages with the fastest current and least resistance and by using only those strokes which accelerate, that is, minimizing the use of stern sweeps and braces. Control and balance in the relatively unstable WW racing hulls are essential.

Follow the dark tongue of the mainstream current.

Follow the flow of the deepest water and avoid shallows with their reduced flow velocity.

Avoid rollers, high standing waves, breakers and haystacks.

Cut through rollers at high speed and at right angles to the length of the roller.

Cut corners to the *inside* of the highest waves, but avoid the shear zone and back-eddy.

It is often more efficient and less tiring to paddle hard and accelerate on the downhill (downstream) slope of high standing waves.

The WW Slalom Course

The course is 600 to 800 m long with 15 to 30 gates suspended over a current of not less than 2 m / sec. The gates are between 1.20 and 3.50 m wide and are suspended high enough to avoid interference by the current and the waves.

Gates are strategically placed so that good WW tactics allow the paddler to utilize currents advantageously. *Power* gates which require strength only are undesirable. An equal number of left- and right-turn gates ensures that left- or right-handed paddlers are not disadvantaged.

The gates are numbered in the order in which they are to be passed. The green-white pole always hangs on the right, the red-white pole on the left. *Forward* gates are entered bow-first, *reverse* gates stern-first and *upstream* gates bow-first from the downstream side. In addition, these gates may be straight (aligned at right angles to the current), *oblique* (aligned at an angle to the current), *offset* (out of line with the previous gate), or *flush* (two gates formed by 3 poles, the middle pole being common to both). *Team* gates are specially marked for team competition.

WW Slalom Rules

1. Gates must be passed in correct order and in the direction indicated by the poles (i.e., green-white on the right, red-white on the left).
2. Both bow and stern must pass cleanly through the *vertical plane* between the poles. However, there is no penalty given for a boat end which ''sneaks'' under one of the poles without touching.
3. The boat must pass through the gate in an *upright* position.
4. Gates may not be touched by boat, paddle, or any part of the paddler's body, or penalty points are awarded.
5. For team gates, all 3 boats must pass through the gate within 15 seconds.
6. Competitors who capsize on the course and are unable to roll back up are automatically disqualified.
7. The course is run *twice* with the better run counted as the final score.
8. The score is tabulated by adding the time on the course in *seconds* with the *number* of penalty points accumulated. The lowest sum determines the winner.

Penalty Points

0 points for passing through the gate in correct order and direction without touching.

10 points for touching *one* pole on the *inside* with boat, paddle or body.

20 points for touching *both* poles on the *inside* or *one* pole on the *outside* and subsequently passing through the gate.

50 points for
- Intentionally pushing a pole aside to facilitate passage.
- Rolling in the gate (whether the body is ahead of or behind the plane).
- Passing through the gate in the wrong direction (i.e., with wrong boat end or from wrong side).
- Completely missing a gate without touching and entering the next gate.
- Making a repeated attempt at the gate *after* the body has broken the plane between the poles. Repeated attempts may be made without penalty if the plane has not been broken by the body and neither pole has been touched.

WW Slalom Tactics

Trial runs are not always permitted on WW slalom courses; therefore, careful reconnoitering of the course is especially important. Plan the tactics for each gate from shore, but be prepared to improvise on the water.

The first run should be aimed at completing the *entire* course for a reasonable score but without taking unnecessary chances. The experiences of this run may be used to alter the tactics and improve technique on the second run.

In addition, it is often advantageous to observe the techniques used by other paddlers on the course. Use the techniques that worked for them and avoid making the same mistakes.

Align the craft far enough upstream for proper bow- or stern-first passage. Plan ahead.

Use back-eddies for approaching upstream gates and when working upstream for a second attempt at a gate which has been missed.

Whenever possible, use strokes which *accelerate* and *maintain* speed (e.g., cut quickly across the current for an offset gate, rather than back-paddling and ferrying).

Chapter 4　Flat Water Racing

FW racing is a test of paddling strength and endurance. The aim is to cover *standard* distances in the shortest time. FW racing shells must conform to regulation length, width, shape and weight. The ideal regatta course has between 8 and 10 lanes, no current, and minimal wave formation and is sheltered from wind — especially side-winds. Artificial man-made regatta courses are therefore preferred for top-level international competition.

K-2

C-1

EVENTS

Olympic FW racing consists of seven events:

Men's   1000 m K-1, K-2, K-4, C-1
                and C-2
Women's   500 m K-1 and K-2

At world championships and local regattas, additional events are usually staged:

Men's   10 000 m K-1, K-2, K-4,
                 C-1 and C-2
         5000 m K-1, K-2, K-4,
                 C-1 and C-2
         500 m K-1 and C-1
         500 m Sprint relay for
                 K-1 and some-
                 times K-1 + K-2
                 + C-1 + C-2
         1000 m War canoe
         1000 m C-4
Women's   500 m K-4 and War
                 canoe

War Canoe   C-4

Due to variable water conditions (wind, waves, and sometimes currents), standard or record times are representative values only. The winner is always chosen by a series of elimination heats, repêchages, semi-finals and the final. Representative times of the top paddlers today are:

Event	500 m	1000 m	10 000 m
Men's K-1	under 1:55 min	*ca.* 3:50 min	under 43:00 min
K-2		*ca.* 3:30 min	*ca.* 38:00 min
K-4		*ca.* 3:10 min	under 36:00 min
C-1	*ca.* 2:00 min	*ca.* 4:15 min	under 50:00 min
C-2		under 4:00 min	under 45:00 min
Women's K-1	*ca.* 2:00 min		
K-2	*ca.* 1:55 min		

K-4

Kayak

Torso and shoulder are rotated forward strongly and the arm is extended fully for maximum reach.

The blade is dropped quickly and immersed *completely* for the entry before main pull is initiated.

Pull is initiated by the powerful back muscles. Torso and shoulder are rotated back forcefully.

Simultaneously, the leg on the stroke side is extended, stemming strongly against the stem-board to stabilize the hip for maximum force transmission.

FW RACING TECHNIQUE

FW racing technique reflects the paddler's attempts to maximize the propulsive force of each stroke and to minimize non-productive effort. High stroke rate (strokes / minute), smoothly coordinated stroke rhythm, and efficient style are the keystones to good performance.

Power of torso rotation is transmitted to the immersed blade by the extended (straight wrist) stroke arm for the pull.

The upper arm complements with some straightening and stabilizes the paddle for good blade position (vertical and close to keel-line) throughout the pull.

Recovery is inititated at hip level (elbow at right angles — not smaller).

Forearm and wrist are quickly flexed up (elbow and shoulder stay *low*) and the extended recovery arm is simultaneously dropped for the next stroke.

Canoe

The paddler's weight remains centred over the kneeling leg.

For a maximum reach, the upper-body weight is thrown forward onto the blade.

The upper arm complements with some straightening and stabilizes the paddle for good blade position throughout the pull.

A simultaneous strong righting of the upper body generates maximum pull on the shaft.

Recovery is initiated at hip level. The blade is sliced sideways and out, angled to cut into the wind, and swung

Pull is initiated by the back muscles as torso, shoulder and extended arm are forcefully rotated back.

forward for the next stroke. Arms and hands are relaxed.

FW RACING TACTICS

FW races are won by fast *starts,* maintainance of *pace* in the middle of the race and strong *finishing sprints.* In 500 and 1000 m events, the straightest course is the fastest. Leaving your lane or intentionally ''riding the wash'' (sliding forward on the bow wave) of other boats results in automatic disqualification. In 5000 and 10 000 m races, it is often advantageous to ride the wash of the boat ahead to conserve energy. Towards the finish (or at a strategic moment when the other crew tires and slows the pace) sprint off the wash and try to pass your opponent quickly (to make him drop back *behind* your wash).

On the circular 5000 and 10 000 m courses, use strong leans and wide bow sweeps to enhance the turning effect ▶ while maintaining speed. If possible, cut to the *inside* of other competitors at the turn buoy to reduce the turning radius.

To help maintain or pick up the pace, some paddlers regularly intersperse series of 10, 20 or more very powerful strokes at strategic points throughout the race distance.

Good pacing over the race distance is very important and often determines the outcome. However, a paddler's pacing depends on his individual strengths and weaknesses. Some paddlers have fast starts but are weak at the finish. Others gain what was lost at the start in the middle of the race. Finally, there are some who come ''out of nowhere'' to beat the entire field with a tremendous finishing sprint. Experience and *tempo-training* will help the paddler use his strengths and improve on his weaknesses to determine his pacing and allow him to ''run his own race'' with confidence.

TRAINING FOR FW RACING

The key to success in FW racing competition is a long-term and well-planned training programme. To achieve top-level performance in international competition, FW racing athletes train with *graduated* intensity over a period of years. Training phases and individual sessions are designed and scheduled to attain specific improvements over a period of time.

Good training programmes are based on physiologically- and psychologically-sound principles and aim to gradually improve and finally maximize the qualities of paddling strength, endurance, stamina and power.

The yearly training cycle is divided into phases, each of which relies on the previous phase(s) to attain its specific goals. There is no abrupt separation between phases, but rather a diminution of one training emphasis with a corresponding increase in the next. Needless to say, the programme must be flexible enough to allow the *retention* of specific qualities through various phases. Cardiorespiratory endurance and muscle strength, for instance, are best maintained during the competitive season by continued running and weight training.

In general, the phases are:
1. FOUNDATION: build-up of all-round organic fitness
2. FORMATION: build-up of paddling fitness
3. COMPETITION: development and maintainance of top paddling form and peaking for the most important event(s)
4. TRANSITION: gradual tapering of paddling training intensity
5. ACTIVE REST: low intensity all-round training

Fitness is best achieved by an effective dry land training programme which provides a varied and interesting combination of running, swimming, cycling and cross-country skiing to develop cardiorespiratory endurance; calisthenics, gymnastics, athletics (track & field), games (e.g., soccer, basketball, volleyball, handball) for general coordination, flexibility, agility and balance; and weight training to maximize muscular strength, endurance and power.

Specific paddling fitness is best achieved by on-the-water training using the principles of:

Fartlek training (speed play). Long distances are covered using a varied pace to develop muscular endurance and some speed.

Over-distance training. Distances greater than the length of the actual race are covered at a slower pace than in the event (with sufficient rest for complete recovery between repeats) to develop muscular endurance.

Under-distance training. Short distances are covered at a faster pace than in the event (with complete recovery between repeats) to develop speed and a feeling for pacing or tempo.

Interval training. Specific distances (never over event distance) are covered at a specific pace (slower than race or maximum pace) with a controlled amount of rest (incomplete recovery between repeats) to develop specific cardiorespiratory and muscular endurance.

Sprint training. Short distances are covered at maximum pace (with complete recovery between repeats) to develop speed, specific muscular strength and stamina (staying power).

When training on waters without exact distance markings, *time* is substituted for distance and *stroke rate* for pace.

Distance	Approximate time equivalent	
	C-1	K-1
50 m	00:15 min	00:12 min
100 m	00:30 min	00:25 min
200 m	1:00 min	00:50 min
300 m	1:30 min	1:15 min
500 m	2:20 min	1:55 min
800 m	3:45 min	3:15 min
1000 m	4:30 min	4:00 min
3000 m	15:00 min	12:20 min.
5000 m	25:00 min	20:00 min
10 000 m	55:00 min	43:00 min

Pace	Approximate stroke rate equivalent	
	C-1	K-1
10 000 m race pace	55 — 60 per min	90 — 100 per min
1000 m	63 — 68 per min	105 — 115 per min
Short sprints (15 seconds)	70 — 80 per min	120 + per min

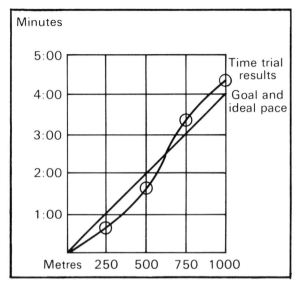

Each training session (on both water and land) is also divided into phases which allow a gradual adjustment of mind and body to the workload.

1. Warm-up: running, stretching exercises and light calisthenics on land.
2. Build-up: distance paddling at slow to moderate pace with a gradual increase of training intensity.
3. Work: specific high intensity training with maximum effort.
4. Transition: diminution of training intensity.
5. Cool-off: relaxed, slow paddling, loosening-up exercises on land, stowing equipment, showers, massage.

Special attention and consideration is given to perfection of *technique* and *tactics* during all water training sessions, particularly in the early and late phases of the yearly training cycle where distance paddling predominates. Race tactics (e.g., riding wash, turns, pacing) are also developed and continually improved throughout the competition phase.

Throughout the paddling season, individual time-trials and competition results may be used to determine a paddler's specific weaknesses. When times are plotted on a graph as shown, the deviation from the ideal race pace is easily seen. The results here demonstrate excess speed over the first 500 m, followed by loss of staying power and a poor final time. This paddler's training sessions must now concentrate on tempo training to improve pacing over the first 500 m and interval training to improve endurance for the latter half of the race.

Chapter 5   Touring

PORTAGING

Most extended paddling tours involve some carrying of craft and equipment overland. Contrary to first impressions, portaging is a most important skill for wilderness travel. With a little foresight and planning, it provides an interesting diversion from endless paddling. Otherwise, portaging inevitably becomes sheer drudgery. Therefore, before loading the kitchen sink on top of all the other comforts of home into the boat, consider the following:

Portages should be covered on *one* trip. Numerous heavy or unmanageable pieces of equipment plus a heavy craft require back-tracking which can be a time-consuming and energy-robbing experience. Therefore, minimize *weight* and *volume.*

Choose the lightest craft suitable for the tour (e.g., a P-F canoe or kayak).

Choose the lightest and least voluminous basic equipment (e.g., lightweight back-packing tents, down-filled sleeping bags, light-weight aluminum cooking utensils, down clothing and light footwear, light nylon shell rainwear).

Avoid heavy canned foods. Special dehydrated foods are fine, though the lighter they are, the more they seem to cost. A little ingenuity combined with basic cooking skills can usually turn everyday kitchen staples into reasonable substitutes.

Choose the lightest, strongest and most voluminous packs (i.e., the frameless Hudson's Bay packs with tumpline are especially suited to touring by open canoe).

Reduce the equipment to basic necessities and pack everything into as few packs as possible. Distribute the weight per pack so that the load is proportional to the strength and capability of the carrier (e.g., for a one to two week tour, a crew of three in a P-F touring canoe should manage with two Hudson's Bay packs and perhaps one smaller pack for the person carrying the canoe).

If back-tracking is unavoidable (on long tours with heavier or more numerous packs), carry a load for 6 to 8 minutes, then place it beside the trail and head back for the second, and so on. This shuttle system avoids overexertion with heavy loads and allows time to recover during the hike back.

When touring by kayak or other decked craft, back-tracking is usually unavoidable due to the use of smaller, more numerous packs.

Touring by canoe and kayak is a healthy, adventurous and enjoyable form of recreation. Extended over days or weeks by camping en route, a paddling tour can lead through remote wilderness areas which are difficult, if not impossible, to reach by any other means. Many of the paddling, portaging, camping, cooking, wilderness travel and route-finding techniques — as well as the routes themselves — used in North America today have been inherited from the native peoples and early explorers of this continent. In a sense then, touring our countless interconnecting waterways and endless shorelines is also a journey into the past. It takes man back into a time and atmosphere of challenge and high adventure, and it provides a source of invaluable cultural and historical insight.

Above all, the *feeling* of freedom and self-sufficiency derived from meeting the challenge of a wilderness paddling tour is a rare experience in this modern age and can help establish a deep sense of appreciation for the real beauty and spirit of the natural environment.

Portaging the canoe:

The hands are evenly spaced on each side of the yoke. The arms are comfortably extended and the hull rests against the thighs. Knees are bent for balance.

The knees are momentarily straightened, then bent and thrust forward strongly as the hands depress the gunwale. The hull tilts on its edge and the hand in front of the yoke quickly reaches over to grasp the far gunwale.

The arm on the near gunwale slides under the side of the hull so that the gunwale rests in the crook of the elbow. Again, the knees are momentarily straightened, then bent and thrust forward strongly as the hull is rolled upside-down overhead, and the head and shoulders are brought under the yoke with a ¼ turn.

To roll the canoe down, the same procedure is followed in reverse.

With practice, the canoe can be easily rolled up and down with a minimum of lifting. The knee-thrust adds *momentum* to the hull and the *low* stance allows the paddler to position himself appropriately under the hull, rather than lifting the hull into position overhead.

A canoe without a yoke is carried by resting the centre-thwart on one shoulder and across the upper back. For increased comfort, two paddles may be lashed to the centre-thwart and

the bow seat. The blades are lashed to the thwart with enough space between for the head. The flat blade area rests on the shoulders. To save time, the lashing is left permanently attached and the paddles are slipped into place for the portage.

C-1 and K-1 closed hulls are best carried by hanging the boat over the shoulder by the coaming. C-2 and K-2 hulls are usually too heavy or awkward for one person to carry.

LOADING AND TRIM

For optimum handling of the loaded craft, equipment and paddler(s) must be distributed evenly so that the hull rides on an even keel.

2-man crew   3-man crew

In an open canoe, the packs are placed fore and aft of the centre-thwart or yoke. With a crew of three, the pack behind centre serves as a sitting platform (preferably a ''blanket'' pack with no fragile items). The pack in front is aligned lengthwise to allow room for the feet. A smaller third pack is stowed in front of the stern paddler and it may be shifted for final trim.

The packs are best placed with shoulder harness facing up for handy grip. When lifting packs out, grasp both shoulder straps *and* tumpline close to their attachment and stand the pack up on end first. Renew the grip close to the attachment and then lift. This procedure minimizes strain on individual straps and their attachment.

In decked hulls, the equipment is best packed into smaller bags which fit through the cockpit and which are shaped to fill out the bow and stern holds most efficiently. A removable or hinged seat and removable stem-board are advantageous. Sometimes seat and stem-board are replaced by suitable items of luggage to save weight. Tie-strings fastened to each bag and kept near the cockpit facilitate quick retrieval of equipment from inaccessible bow and stern holds.

For proper trim, smaller, heavier items are stored in the bow of a K-1 and larger, more voluminous gear in the stern. K-2s offer more room between the cockpits. On longer tours, light, bulky excess gear is sometimes fastened on to the deck behind the cockpit.

EMBARKING AND DISEMBARKING

An order to the process of loading and unloading a 2- or 3-man canoe helps avoid confusion, loss of balance and possible upset. In addition to the fundamental embarking and disembarking procedures, the following points are helpful:

One person at a time stows his pack in the appropriate place while the other(s) steadies the boat with *both* hands on the gunwale. At awkward embarkation points, it is often best for one person to board the canoe and, keeping weight low and centred over the keel-line, stow each pack as it is handed aboard from shore. At landings, the last man to disembark hands the equipment ashore.

The loading sequence should be such that an even keel is maintained. When boarding, first the middle, then the bow, and finally the stern paddler assume their positions. At landings, the sequence is reversed.

Often a shallow beach or narrow landing calls for an end-on approach. The shore end of the canoe is drawn close to — but not up on — the shore. Resting one end up on land, logs, or rocks reduces stability and can lead to structural damage when loading the hull.

Depending on whether bow or stern faces out, the bow or stern paddler respectively boards the canoe. Equipment is handed to him as the canoe is steadied by the other paddler, who clamps the shore end between his knees.

The last man to board lifts up on the shore end to clear shallows and, placing one foot over the keel-line, shoves off.

Paddles are never thrown or scattered heedlessly on to the landing. *Place* them out of the way — a broken paddle can ruin a tour.

Kayaks and decked canoes are best landed broadside, parallel to shore. In deep waters, always look for the landing which offers the best broadside approach. In shallow waters or at narrow landings, be prepared to do some wading.

TOURING PACE AND RHYTHM

On any tour, the weakest paddler or crew always sets the pace. In team boats, the bow paddler sets the stroke rate and the others follow his rhythm. A comfortable steady rhythm can be maintained for long periods and ensures good progress. In a canoe, the stern paddler times his steering components appropriately without breaking rhythm or missing a stroke.

On extended tours, changing sides and position in the canoe every half day or so ensures balanced exercise for both sides and contributes to the paddlers' versatility of technique.

NAVIGATION AND WAY-FINDING

A route over chains of lakes and rivers with occasional portages may be complicated by numerous islands, large bays, inlets and unmarked or overgrown trails. The exact route is best laid out on a large scale topographic map (1:50 000) of the area. Alternative routes, campsites and points of nearest habitation should also be noted in case of altered water or weather conditions and emergency.

The map is best kept clean, dry and legible by storing in a clear heavy-grade, waterproof plastic case with the pertinent section facing up. Tied to the top of a pack, gunwale or coaming, it is visible for continuous reference.

To follow a route, the map is aligned in accordance with easily recognized landmarks such as points and heights of land, islands, bays and inlets. By correlating reference points from land to map or vice versa, a good estimate of location and direction can be made. When looking for a small inlet, narrow channel, hidden portage or small campsite along a sinuous shoreline, progress is best measured by counting the points of land and bays appearing on the map and then mentally ticking them off as they are passed. Similarly, size, shape and relative position of islands are good indicators for orientation on island-strewn waters.

On unmarked or overgrown portages, a good compass combined with basic orienteering skills can save many hours — if not days — of mind-boggling "bush-whacking" through dense wilderness.

SAFETY

Swamping or capsizing a heavily laden touring craft can have serious consequences. The weight hampers simple manoeuvring and rescue procedures and the amount of equipment complicates retrieval and recovery. The loss of an important piece of equipment or even the craft itself can lead to severe privation and even loss of life on remote wilderness tours.

The best precaution is to learn paddling fundamentals *before* venturing on a tour and to conscientiously improve paddling skills at every opportunity. However, the best paddler is not immune to upset, especially when over-confidence leads to taking unnecessary chances.

A respect for fundamental safety considerations and competence in basic rescue procedures is the responsibility of every paddler on a tour.

Safety Measures

Every tour member should have an introduction to elemental paddling skills and be in good physical shape before embarking on extended tours. Short ''pre-tours'' are helpful.

Every paddler must be a good swimmer and able to tread water for at least 5 minutes with touring clothes and foot-wear on.

Life-vests add a margin of safety, and one for *each* paddler should be stowed within reach.

A tour should include at least one *experienced* paddler for every two tour members. Knowledge and proven skill in water-safety and life-saving techniques are mandatory.

Each paddler should have clearly defined duties in case of upset (e.g., collecting paddles, retrieving and supporting packs, controlling and emptying the boat). This procedure should be practised.

A wilderness tour should include at least one member experienced and competent in wilderness travel, way-finding and survival techniques.

Once under way, stay within sight and calling distance of other crews. This also applies to portages.

If upset appears unavoidable, eject before swamping or capsizing the hull completely and try to keep the equipment afloat.

If capsized, keep the hull upside-down for buoyancy and as a swimming aid. Hold on to paddles and packs until the hull is emptied and righted or until other crews arrive to help.

In a wind, stay on the leeward side of the hull to prevent its drifting out of reach.

Weather

Weather plays an important role on paddling tours not only from the standpoint of enjoyment, but also from the standpoint of safety. Heavy or prolonged rain can quickly swell rivers and streams into raging torrents. Strong winds, high waves and thunderstorms can cause boats to drift off course, can swamp open canoes and pose the threat of lightning. Cold weather and frigid waters present special problems.

Familiarize yourself with natural weather signs (e.g., cloud formations, wind shifts, temperature fluctuations) and plan the day's paddling according to indications.

Minimize the effects of strong head- or side-winds by paddling in the lee of shorelines, even though this route may be longer.

Stay off open water during lightning storms and stay clear of tall, exposed trees or heights of land.

In cold weather and on frigid waters, wear a wet-suit and / or a life-vest. Stay close to shore and keep a waterproofed set of spare clothing handy.

Avoid setting up camp or leaving craft and equipment in low-lying areas beside streams or rivers. A far-off cloudburst can quickly submerge the most attractive campsite overnight and it is an unpleasant — if not impossible — prospect to walk back from a wilderness paddling tour.

The Repair Kit

An important item in every first-aid kit taken along on a wilderness tour is a roll(s) of wide, waterproof adhesive tape. It can work wonders on any dry hull surface which has been punctured and quickly render it seaworthy again. For longer tours, a P-F repair kit can help patch more extensive damage on most hull surfaces including aluminum and canvas.

RESCUE TECHNIQUES

Emptying the Swamped Hull

The Shake-out

When no other crew is within reach to render assistance on open waters, a swamped canoe may be quickly and efficiently emptied using the shake-out technique.

Swim to the middle of the hull on the leeward side.

Grasp the near gunwale and tilt the hull on its side by pushing the gunwale under.

Natural buoyancy and/or flotation aids in the hull will cause the hull to rise in the water. When maximum height is attained, quickly pull the submerged gunwale above surface. The hull is partly emptied by this manoeuvre.

With hands evenly spaced on both sides of the centre-thwart, grasp the near gunwale. Pull the chest in close to the gunwale.

In a smooth, contiguous movement, dip the near gunwale about one inch under the surface and simultaneously execute a strong horizontal "frog-kick" as the arms straighten to push the hull away.

At the end of the push, sharply lift the gunwale above surface again. Pull the chest in close to the gunwale again and repeat the sequence until the hull is emptied. The hull is in effect being pushed out from under the water.

With practice, the average paddler can empty a standard 16-foot open canoe in less than 20 seconds. With larger canoes, two or three paddlers working in unison along the same gunwale can efficiently empty the hull.

The shake-out can be used with decked hulls with some success. However, the decking and small cockpit opening make it less effective and a considerable amount of water usually remains inside the hull.

The Canoe-over-canoe Rescue

When other crews are within reach, the swamped canoe is quickly and efficiently emptied by this method while the swimmers support equipment and hold on to the bow and stern of the rescue canoe.

The rescue canoe is aligned at right angles to the swamped craft and at one end. The rescuer assumes a *low* position.

The swamped hull is turned upside-down, and the end is lifted on to the gunwale.

The hull is pulled up and across until it rests balanced across both gunwales.

The near gunwale is lifted, and the hull is turned right-side-up to rest balanced across both gunwales.

The emptied hull is slid across the gunwales back into the water.

Getting Back Into the Hull from the Water

In open canoes, climb aboard one at a time while the others steady the canoe at bow and stern. Once aboard, sit or lie down over the keel-line to increase stability as the others climb aboard.

Grasp both gunwales about one-third of the length from one end of the hull.

With a strong frog-kick, pull the body up and across the gunwale while leaning down hard on the far gunwale (elbow high) to keep the near gunwale above water.

Once the hips are over the near gunwale, turn and drop the rear end into the boat. Then swing the legs aboard and assume a low position over the keel-line until all are on board.

Kayaks are boarded from the water by straddling the stern deck, and, keeping the weight low by bending forward at the hips, pulling on the rear coaming and sliding forward until the hips are over the seat. Drop the rear end into the seat and resume position in the cockpit.

TOURING COASTAL WATERS

Paddling along endless miles of ocean or large inland lake coastline offers an interesting and challenging adventure to the touring enthusiast. Coastal waters are usually more accessible than wilderness areas and provide an unlimited yet much neglected paddler's playground.

Surf, spray and whitecaps accompany the winds and swells of expansive open waters. Under these conditions, the Eskimo kayak demonstrates its intended purpose most admirably.

Navigating Coastlines

Fogs, good-weather mist and distance often combine to obscure landmarks and make sightings difficult. A good compass mounted on the bow deck and aligned with the centre-line for sighting purposes can sometimes help to indicate the general heading. However, the relatively slow rate of travel and the susceptibility of the small craft to currents and side-winds make compass travel alone unreliable. For this reason, it is best to stay within sight of the shoreline and use sightings to hold the course indicated by the compass bearing. Especially useful are two prominent landmarks which stand directly in the line of travel and are a good distance apart. When the paddler is straying off course, the landmarks appear to move further apart, indicating the need for a course correction.

Tidal *ebb* and *flow* involve strong offshore and onshore currents respectively. In narrow channels between islands, in fiords and at the mouths of rivers, these currents are especially strong and capricious. Since currents of this magnitude cannot be overcome by paddling, *marine charts* and *tidal calendars* for the area must be studied. Landings and launchings can be timed appropriately to take best advantage of onshore currents and to avoid strong offshore currents.

Paddling Technique in High Swells

Best progress can be made when travelling with the swells in a *tail wind*. By paddling hard on the downward slope of a swell, the craft can be made to ''surf'' over long stretches at high speed.

When paddling into the wind, a head-on approach into swells is usually most efficient, although very high waves with short periods often result in a rough, spine-jarring ride and the hull tends to plough. Reduced forward speed and unweighting of the bow (by leaning backward) can minimize these effects.

When ploughing through very high breakers, the weight (force) of the water against the paddler's chest can upset the craft. The tight cockpit and high coaming of original Eskimo kayaks could theoretically break the paddler's back if a powerful breaker forced his torso back on to the stern deck. The Greenland Eskimos avoided this danger with an Eskimo roll. The breaker thus crashed over the hull bottom and the paddler rolled back up once the wave had passed over.

For these reasons, high waves and breakers are often best taken at a slight angle (quartered) and the spray is reduced by ''rolling with the wave'' (i.e., leaning to expose the hull bottom to the oncoming wave) and bracing appropriately.

Paddling in swells invariably results in a wet ride, and a wet-suit or rain shell is mandatory in cold, windy weather.

For optimum speed and efficiency, it is always better to paddle hard on the downward slope and to save energy on the upward slope of the swells.

Safety Measures

Coastal travel involves paddling for long, uninterrupted stretches. Good physical condition and a measure of paddling endurance are prerequisites for long tours.

Shorelines are often too far distant to reach by swimming. To minimize trouble in the event of upset, perfect the Eskimo roll.

Before embarking, examine the hull, steering mechanism and cables, spray-skirt and paddle for signs of weakness or wear. Repair or replace defective items immediately.

A life-vest and spare paddle within easy reach are standard equipment.

Brightly coloured life-vests, jackets and hulls of red or orange are easily spotted on vast expanses of water. The bow deck, however, should be a dark, matte colour to reduce glare.

Plan and map out the route on marine charts. Calculate an average of 15 to 20 miles per day and make certain that every tour member can maintain this pace. Also note alternative routes to be used in the event of strong winds.

Collect up-to-date weather information from marine forecasts and locals. Head- or side-winds above a reading of 3 on the Beaufort scale (above 12 m.p.h.) can prevent making headway or blow the paddler far off course.

Inform the Coast Guard or local authorities of your planned route and the duration of the tour. Then, stick to these plans.

Coastal areas are usually frequented by other traffic. Stay clear of shipping lanes. Get off the water before nightfall or when fogs reduce visibility below safe limits. Include a loud whistle, a bright signal lamp and flares with the equipment when on extended tours along busy coastlines.

Launch and land in sheltered areas such as behind break-walls. In surf, launch head-on into breakers and land head-on to shore.

Stay as close to the shoreline as breakers and turbulence from reflected waves permit.

Travel point-to-point and in the lee of the wind when possible. Be prepared to land if head-winds or offshore winds prove too strong.

Under cold conditions, wear a wet-suit or waterproof wind shell plus the life-vest. Neoprene gloves, or "sleeves" which are attached to the shaft of the paddle, keep wet fingers comfortable in cold and wind.

Ultra-violet radiation is very intense on open waters, even under a cloud cover. Wear a hat and sunglasses and keep sensitive parts of the body covered.

Try to keep the hands dry. Constantly wet hands become desiccated causing the skin to crack open. These cracks are especially painful in salt water. Rubber cupped rings on the neck of a double-blade paddle reduce the flow of water down the shaft.

Campsites and mooring points for the boats should be chosen well above high tide levels.

Choose campsites with a *fresh water* source. If long stretches with uncertain drinking water availability are anticipated, carry a sufficient quantity in the boat.

If ejection should be necessary following an upset, keep the hull upside-down and slip out of the spray-skirt *without* releasing it from the coaming. Now hold the waistband of the spray-skirt closed and quickly roll the hull upright so that minimum water is shipped.

Stay on the leeward side of the hull and hold on to the paddle. (Some paddlers prefer to secure the paddle to the hull by means of a long cord. However, this method is *unsafe* in fast currents and turbulent water where the paddler may become entangled in the line.)

Get back into the boat by straddling the stern deck and sliding forward over the cockpit.

If a second crew is close enough to render quick assistance, they can help the capsized paddler *roll* back up by
— approaching the capsized hull so that the boats are parallel, the cockpits adjacent, and the hulls about 3 feet apart,
— placing the paddle across both hulls to span the distance between them,
— guiding the capsized paddler's hands to the horizontal shaft.

The capsized paddler now pulls himself up on the shaft, righting the hull.